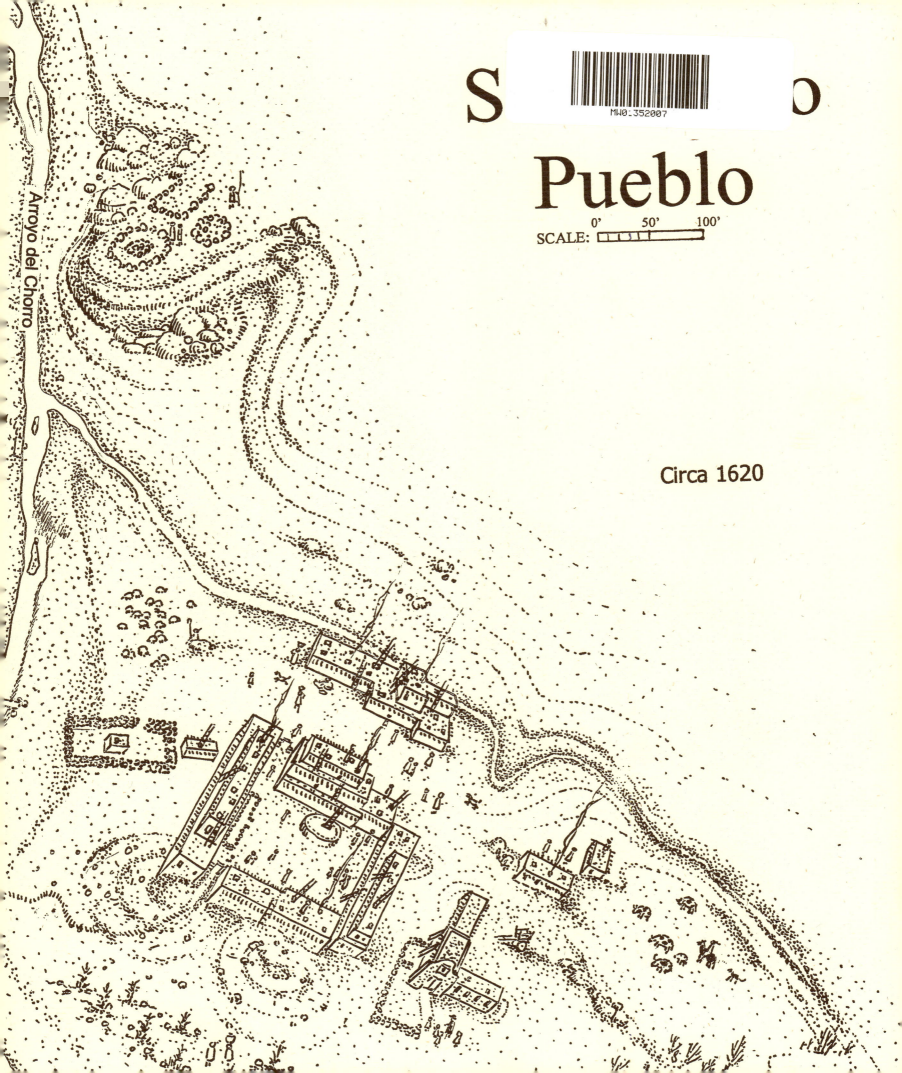

THE SECRETS OF
SAN LAZARO PUEBLO

FORREST FENN

SPECIAL POTTERY SECTION BY FRANCIS HARLOW AND DWIGHT LANMON

*If you love the lore and the lure
of ancient places and things, this volume
is dedicated to you. May the stories herein
keep you forever asking and searching.*

THIS FIRST EDITION IS LIMITED TO 2000 COPIES.

NUMBER 1283 .

Forrest Fenn (signature)

Cover painting by James Asher
Title page illustration by Carole Gardner

Published by One Horse Land & Cattle Co.
P.O. Box 8174
Santa Fe, NM 87501
ffenn@earthlink.net
Copyright © 2004 Forrest Fenn
ISBN 0-9670917-2-1

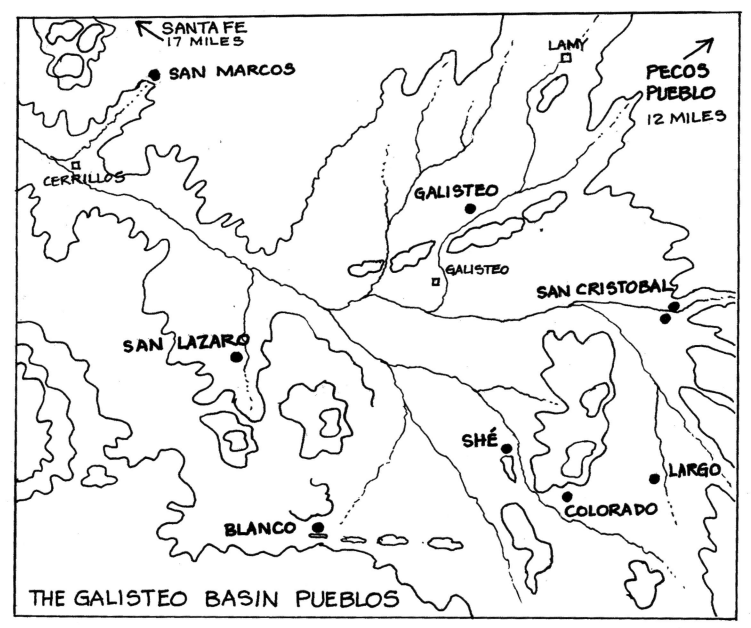

Figure 1   Carole Gardner

PREFACE

Although the preparation of this book was assisted by a host of competent and dedicated professional archaeologists, our targeted readers are those who possess only a casual knowledge of ancient sites and visit the museums of the world mostly because they love to look at objects. If we had our way, you would be able to touch any ancient artifact in any museum. To see an Anasazi bowl in a glass display case may bring a few rewards, but to hold that vessel, to feel its weight, to smell its smells, or to study the wear on its bottom would evoke a whole new spectrum of knowledge and understanding. So, even though we may not be able to hand you a pottery bowl, we hope to bring you much closer to it than you have been before.

A sparse few will berate this effort for its lack of metric measurements, footnotes, references, bibliography, computer graphics, and the bewilderment of archaeospeak. In fact, this book was written mostly just for the fun of doing it and to experience the exhilaration that comes from speaking about a subject we love in a simple, main-street prose. We lack any ambition to be technically dull, nor do we crave the accolades of those who will surely find fault with our processes. We believe the greater part of knowledge is knowing those things not worthy of knowing.

Because we believe that archaeology is not quite an exclusive science, we promote a contrary claim that its real value is in the vast reservoir of human interest stories that the earth divulges through those like us who cut the roots, lift the rocks, and screen the dirt.

My partner in this project is Charmay Allred, who is largely devoid of the major flaws that plague even the best of humankind, and who, instead, is blessed with a vast array of social graces and wonderment for editing, wordsmithing, and conjuring up the ideas that have made this labor feasible. She relishes her additional duty of being docent for the diverse collection of artifacts in our lab, where she encourages all visitors to pick up and examine anything that strikes their curious minds. At San Lazaro Pueblo, Charmay has been the tour director for hundreds of would-have-been archaeologists and historians who are eager to see and learn from someone who knows most of the plants, the rocks, and the artifacts by name. Together we share the little One Horse Land and Cattle Company, which has published this volume. Call it a vanity book, and you will have it figured out.

We have decided to say what we wish in a conversational tone as we look at the objects from San Lazaro and consider the mysteries and secrets that surround them. So, if you have an open mind and a romantic bent, please pull up a cushioned chair and come in a little closer. We will try to hand you something.

Barton Wright

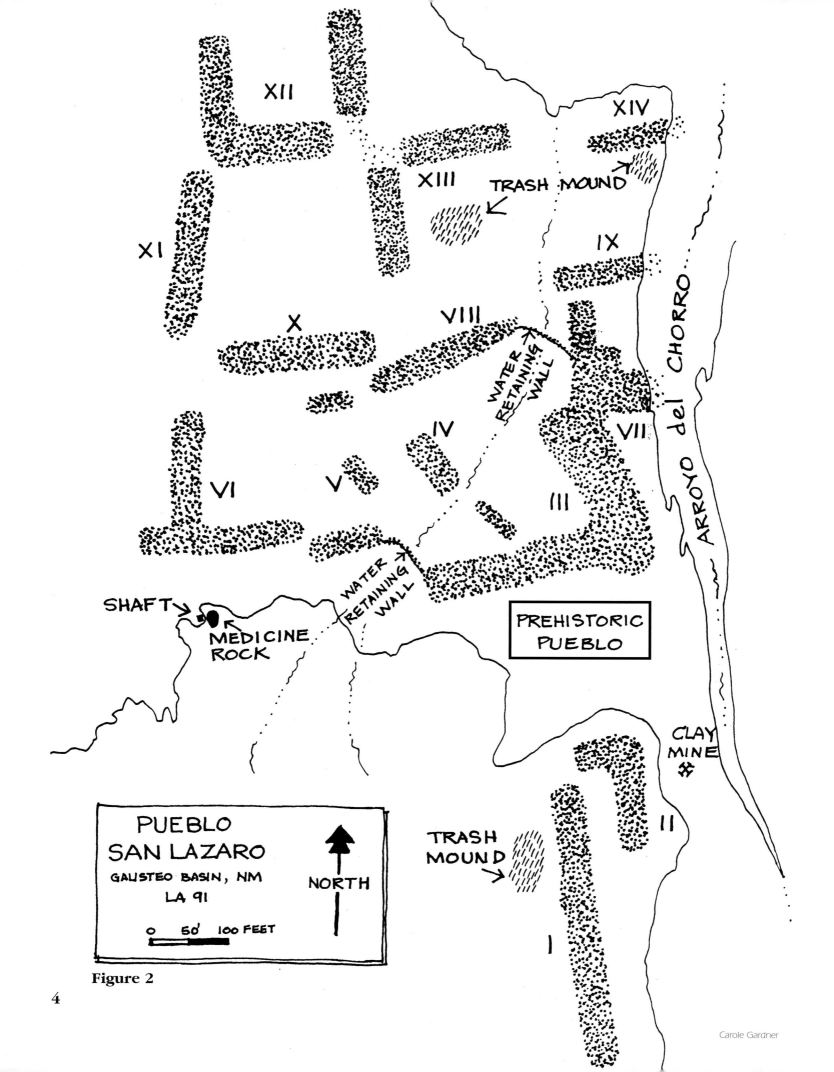

Figure 2

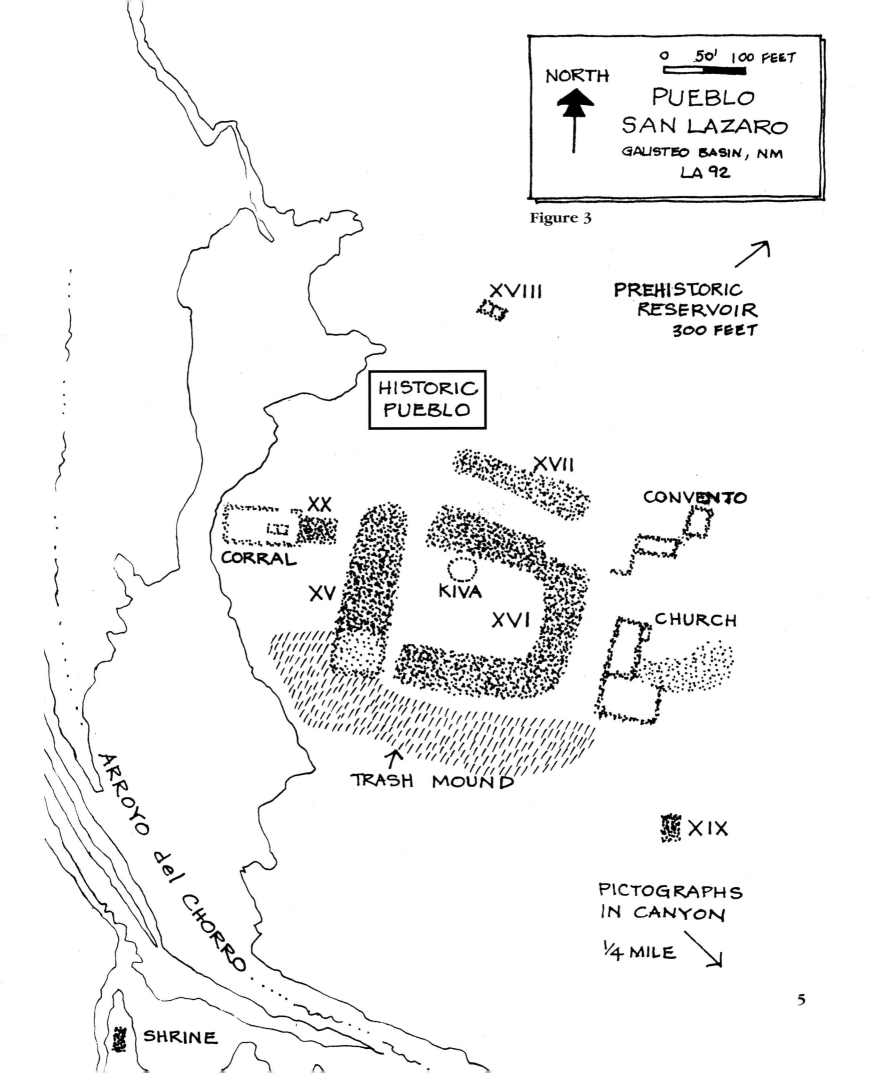

Figure 3

Plate 1

This photo, which shows part of the prehistoric side of the pueblo with long, morning tree shadows, was taken by Paul Logsdon from his airplane in about 1984. The road at the bottom comes in from the north, curls east in between Buildings X on the left and VI on the right, and finally stops at Building VII. The lazy Del Chorro Creek ambles across the top. If this picture could have been taken 500 years earlier, you might have seen 800 Indians in the view. Smoke from breakfast fires would have been coming from some of the buildings, dogs and turkeys would have been running around looking for scratch, and the landscape would have been mostly devoid of vegetation.

Plate 2

An aerial view shows the rooms we have excavated in both the north end of Building I (in the center of the picture) and the smaller Building II (near the top). We backfilled some rooms and saved the south half of each building for future archaeologists to excavate. Most of the artifacts we have recovered have come from these two roomblocks.

" . . . and the end of all of our exploring will be to arrive where we started, and know it for the first time."

T. S. Eliot

THE MAGIC

"The Spirits are all around us." That's what the Tewa elder murmured as we wandered through the stone and adobe ruins of San Lazaro Pueblo. He spoke with such deep feeling and eloquence that I could almost feel the spirits' presence. It was in May of 1993 when we had met and talked at the site. "I am sure my people are from this place," he said, "but of another time, long, long ago." It had been 316 years to be exact, when most of the Tewas had abandoned this pueblo and eventually moved to the village of Hano on the Hopi reservation in Arizona, while a few of the families remained located along the Santa Cruz River north of Santa Fe. The elder, who was pleased that we were working on this book, said, "Be sure and tell them the spirits are happy with you." I promised we would.

If you visited the site today, you might fail to recognize it among the rolling piñon-and-juniper-spotted hills of the Galisteo Basin, eighteen miles southeast of Santa Fe, New Mexico. Only cholla-covered mounds of stone and sandy soil remain of what was once a sprawling apartment complex. No intact structures are visible now to hint that centuries ago this was a beautifully placed village that was cradled in along the trickle of Del Chorro Creek, where an enormous sky still surrounds an endless reach of land and rock.

The Galisteo Basin is home to eight large pueblo ruins (see figure 1) of which San Lazaro, a Tano pueblo, is the largest. Some archaeologists think there may be as many as 5,000 rooms in its twenty-seven roomblocks that cover more than fifty-seven acres. It is a huge site measuring 1,438 feet north to south and 1,738 feet east to west. What is now only silence occasionally broken by the forlorn wail of a lonely coyote or the baraank of a passing raven, was once a bustling city that may have been home to 1,800 or more people at one time.

EARLY OCCUPANTS

About 1150 AD, a few temporary tenants built pithouses along the creek, most of which have been covered by debris falling from later-constructed buildings. Although those earliest inhabitants have been largely ignored and forgotten, the stories of their lives are vital to the history of San Lazaro. Hopefully future archaeologists will be able to uncover their history.

The first stone and adobe rooms built at San Lazaro were constructed in the last part of the twelfth century in Buildings VII and IX (see figure 2, page 4). Because many of those dwellings were later washed away by flash flooding, today it is impossible to identify the full extent of their original construction. During the monsoon season, the barely flowing Del Chorro Creek can become a raging deluge that, on one occasion, we measured to be 17 feet high.

In the fourteenth century, the swirling water was high enough to wash 18 inches of gravel into some of the rooms on the east end of Building VIII. No matter about that, the inhabitants apparently moved right back in on top of the gravel and went on with their lives as if nothing had happened.

Barton Wright

Plate 3

DEL CHORRO CREEK

Del Chorro Creek is a stream that flows intermittently and goes underground at San Lazaro. Running water can be seen in this photo that faces north along the canyon toward the pueblo, two miles distant. The high canyon walls end a short distance south of where this photo was made, as the terrain flattens into gently rolling hills. Igneous rocks that fell from these bluffs and were washed downstream were used as building materials. On the distant right horizon, the Sangre de Cristo Mountains stand guard over the valley.

In 1912, archaeologist Nels Nelson took the photo below looking north down Del Chorro Creek along the east side of the prehistoric pueblo. Water can be seen flowing along the bank, and a lone tepee stands at far left near Building III. Trees and other vegetation have not yet returned in any abundance, even 322 years after San Lazaro was abandoned. The barrenness suggests that the Indians may have had to walk two miles or more in order to obtain firewood.

Neg. No. 15948, Courtesy Department of Library Services, American Museum of Natural History.

Figure 4

Plate 4

Water from Del Chorro Creek departs the swimming hole and flows north over a large, submerged sandstone boulder, only to disappear later into the sandy bottom of the streambed. In wetter years, it might flow another 400 feet before it sinks into the sand.

Engineers William Turney and William Sundt estimated that the water in the creek flows at the rate of ten to fifteen gallons a minute or 14,400 to 21,600 gallons a day. Estimating an average flow of 18,000 gallons a day, half of which might have been collected during a twelve-hour workday, each of 2,000 inhabitants would have had 2.25 gallons of water to use. During years of drought, the population of the pueblo was determined by how much drinking water was available.

THE SWIMMING HOLE

Plate 5

The swimming hole at San Lazaro looked like this in the summer of 1996. On many occasions, after a long, hot day of excavating, I have jumped out of my dirty, sweaty, smelly clothes and waded into the cool waters of this special pool, to enjoy the solitude that has been so important to me. I have sat in the muddy bottom, with water up to my chest, and rested my weary back against the sandstone shelf that is partly submerged.

The nesting pair of bald eagles that live up the canyon have come by to say hello, as small water snakes have busied themselves trying to catch the many tadpoles that populated the summer water all around me. Mule deer, coyotes, mountain lions, bears, the quirky killdeer, and a host of smaller animals and birds have left their footprints in the sand where they have stood to drink.

For centuries, the large rock extended completely across the creek and dammed the gently moving water. When sudden summer thunderstorms swelled the stream, the rushing water hit the rock outcrop with great force and was deflected up, only to come crashing down to erode away the sand on the other side and carry it downstream, leaving a deeper pool. If the storm was smaller, the slower-moving water brought sand and small pebbles with it, filling the pool to a shallower depth. So this little swimming hole has seen many changes.

Over the centuries, the winter snows melted and water seeped into the porous sandstone. At night the water froze, expanded, and slowly flaked away the surface of the stone, until now it spans only one-third of the creek bottom. The revered swimming hole, where thousands of Indian children must once have frolicked in the soothing water, is now mostly filled with sand, and the unhurried current bypasses the rock on its way to join Galisteo Creek.

Carole Gardner

THE RESERVOIR

Plate 6

Remains of the prehistoric earthen reservoir, located about 300 feet northeast of Building XVI, look like this. Turney and Sundt, who made a comprehensive study of the feature, determined that the dam is 146 feet long and less than 2 feet high today as the result of almost 3 feet, 3 inches of silt that has washed in over the centuries. They calculated the area of the drainage to be 3.2 acres.

Although sufficient information is not available to compute the original capacity of the reservoir, they estimated the present capacity to be 46,700 gallons, and that the reservoir would not hold water for more than two or three weeks.

Because the area around the reservoir is littered with pot sherds, Turney and Sundt assumed that water probably was being carried from the reservoir to irrigate nearby crops, especially corn, which grows well in sandy soil. They state in their report:

> Assuming that reservoir water was used for watering crops, it would have been taken from the reservoir during the growing season. The last killing frost occurs about May 15, and the earliest killing frost occurs around October 20, which means an average of 150 to 160 frost-free days. An average rainfall during the growing season is 7.75 inches. Due to the very high percolation of soil in the drainage area, it is estimated that only 40 percent of the precipitation in the drainage area reaches the reservoir. Once stored in the reservoir, evaporation and percolation further deplete the available water. Thus it is estimated that only 80 percent of the stored water could be used.

They further report that:

> A total of 32 diagnostic pottery rim sherds were collected from the ground surface immediately downstream from the reservoir. All ceramic glaze groups from A to F (1340-1700) are represented, but not equally. Four vessel forms are represented—bowl, shouldered bowl, soup plate, and large jar or olla. The large jar form is most frequent, accounting for 53.1 percent of all rims collected. The Glaze A group accounts for 50 percent of all rim sherds. Rims of Cieneguilla Glaze-on-yellow (1375 to 1425) amounted to 37.5 percent of the assemblage. It is estimated that either the reservoir was built ca.1400 or else that was the time when it was most intensively used.

Plate 7

CLAY BELL

Figure 5

This little prehistoric clay bell, with a hole for hanging, was recovered from the floor of a room in Building I. Its round clapper is also clay. Was it originally sewn on a garment or worn around the neck? Three other similar clay bells were also recovered in broken condition.

Life-size drawing by Carole Gardner.

THE FIRST ARCHAEOLOGY

The first archaeologist to visit San Lazaro was Adolph Bandelier who, in the 1890s, published a brief description of the historic side of the pueblo. Then, in 1912, Nels C. Nelson, an archaeologist working for the American Museum of Natural History in New York, excavated about sixty rooms at the site. To him, the place looked pretty bleak, so he referred to it as an "eroded, treeless depression." When he was there, 232 years after the pueblo had been abandoned, the nearby forested areas and other burnable foliage had not yet recovered from over four centuries of heavy use.

Nelson produced a fairly accurate map of the site in which he distinguished between five historic and twenty-one prehistoric buildings in the village. We admire Nelson's tenacity considering the conditions under which he worked. Although Nelson and his wife were on their honeymoon, they were constantly on the move, traveling in a one-horse, covered surrey among seven pueblos in the Galisteo Basin, all of which were being excavated simultaneously under his direct supervision. He had a number of Mexican laborers employed at each of the sites, which averaged about eight miles apart. Although Nelson's report contained only eight pages about San Lazaro, his astute observations continue to be beneficial.

Barton Wright

MEDICINE ROCK

One of the great mysteries in our investigations is what we refer to as the Medicine Rock. On the extreme western edge of the pueblo and immediately south of Building VI, an unusual globular, eroded, sandstone monolith erupts 18 feet from the earth with such force that it punches a hole right into the sky. Just some 58 feet west of that singular feature, starting at ground level, is a perfectly rectangular shaft, 7 feet, 3 inches by 3 feet, 8 inches that has been chiseled 29 feet, 9 inches straight down into the solid bedrock. Tewa workers must have labored there for months and months, leaving tool marks that are still plain to see.

The 18-foot-high Medicine Rock shows its plaza (east) side with the diagonal tunnel entrance visible at the bottom. Paths in the stone on the back side of this feature make access to the top an easy climb.

Plate

On the far eastern side of the giant face of sandstone, a descending tunnel was dug to meet the vertical shaft at its bottom (see figure 7, next page). Since sandstone is a sedimentary stone laid down by water in layers, it was not possible to create a passage of uniform size, so the tunnel's height varies by as much as 4 feet. The sluffing-off and caving-in of the layered, and sometimes loose, stone must have presented some danger to the workers.

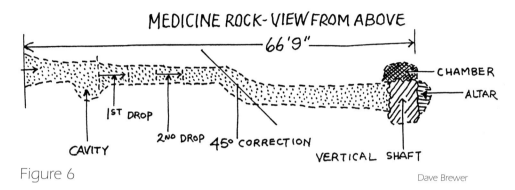

Figure 6
Dave Brewer

It is interesting to note that about halfway down the slanted tunnel, an abrupt, 45-degree right turn made in the construction continues for 4 or 5 feet in that direction before turning left to perfectly align with the bottom of the vertical shaft (see above figure).

The chamber at the bottom, where the tunnel and shaft meet, is 4 feet, 11 inches by 5 feet, 7 inches. Also at the bottom, tucked away under the south wall, is a small alcove or vestibule with a football-shaped, slip-in entrance about 1 foot, 4 inches high. Inside, there is breathing room for six to eight people, the presence of whom could not be visibly detected from the outside.

Franklin Shipla, a Tewa elder who still speaks the ancient language and whose ancestors lived at this pueblo until about 1680, gave the most plausible explanation for the tunnels. He believes great fires were built on each side of the exit facing the plaza as the warriors were descending into the vertical shaft on a rope or ladder, unseen by the assembly waiting on the other side of the Medicine Rock. The shaman stood high above in the saddleback of the rock, dressed in his finery of mountain lion pelt garments and possibly, a feathery headpiece of some sort. Certainly he held ceremonial objects in his hands, perhaps a wand or other articles of great power.

Figure 7

Carole Gardner

As the warriors edged their way up the 66-foot horizontal tunnel to daylight and emerged through the smoke, they were blessed from above with all the power of a strong-willed person's spiritual fervor. All the while the thrilled crowd of relatives, friends, and those whose lives depended on the bravery of the warriors cheered and celebrated the event, "just like at high school pep rallies today," Shipla said with a grin. Some things will never change.

A person descending the horizontal tunnel today and emerging into the light provided by the vertical shaft will see a large pack rat's nest resting on what appears to be an altar that was built into the west wall about 4 feet deep and chest high. The nest is full of cactus spines and an assortment of other materials that give the little critter its name. Our curiosity about the altar is not so great that we have attempted to evict him and his family to investigate. Some secrets are best left alone.

Our guess is that the construction of the tunnel and shaft at the Medicine Rock was completed at the time Roomblock VI was inhabited, which was from about 1330 to 1400. An excavation of the tailings outside of both entrances would reveal broken tools and other artifacts that could more accurately determine the time frame.

Curiously, atop the tailings from the digging of the vertical shaft are hundreds of small (1/2 inch or so in size) pieces of jet, which is a type of lignite. Since jet is not found in sandstone, it could not be part of the construction tailings, and jet has not been found in any other location at the pueblo.

THOUGHTS TO PONDER

1. How was the side chamber at the bottom of the tunnel used?
2. For what purpose were the tunnel and shaft built?
3. Who put the jet on top of the tailings, and why?
4. Was the 45-degree right turn in the horizontal shaft planned so that someone could hide from outside detection, or did the engineer make an error that required correction?

Figure 8

Walter Whitewater, Navajo, blesses the Medicine Rock from where a shaman may have stood 500 years before to bless the ancient warriors as they emerged from the tunnel opening seen below.

Plate 9

Looking Out: Richard Blake sits at the opening of the diagonal tunnel that was constructed through solid sandstone under the Medicine Rock. The steep descent down the 66 feet, 9 inches to the bottom is not too bad if you don't mind the cactus, the bats, the black widow spiders, an occasional rattlesnake, and the pack rats that await your arrival. The journey should not be undertaken without a good flashlight, a stout heart, and someone to go for help if needed. The climb up and out is worse, of course.

Looking In: This flash photograph shows the first few feet of the diagonal tunnel as it disappears into the dark belly of the Medicine Rock.

Plate 10

Plate 11

Looking Down: At the very bottom, where the tunnel and shaft meet under the Medicine Rock, is what appears to be an altar that is partially covered with fall-in rocks and a pack rat's nest.

Looking Up: The symmetry of the vertical shaft is evident in this flash picture that was taken from nearly 30 feet under the Medicine Rock, where the horizontal tunnel joins this shaft. The photographer is standing in front of the altar (see above plate) and adjacent to the side chamber. At the top, the dimensions of this shaft are 7 feet, 3 inches by 3 feet, 8 inches.

Plate 12

BASKET

Plate 13

Near the floor of a room in Building I we discovered this basket, which was abou 6 inches in diameter. A large metate had been inverted on top, but was not touching it. We knew it had been resting there in the dark for over 450 years, so Charmay quickly took its picture, knowing that its life was about to end. When I gently touched the basket, it collapsed into small fragments and was gone.

Many more once-hardy artifacts made from perishable materials still exist in prehistoric contexts, but time is running out. Archaeologists, both professional and amateur, should be more attentive to the necessity of recovering these objects whenever possible. Each artifact that is not recovered is a book that will not be read.

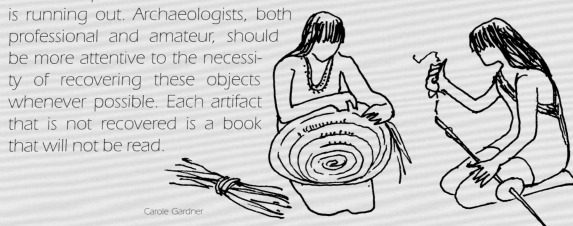

Carole Gardner

VISITING ARCHAEOLOGISTS

During the summers of 1997 and 1998, Michael Gramly, president of the American Society of Amateur Archaeology (ASAA), brought twenty men, women, and youngsters who were society members to San Lazaro to excavate and study. They camped at the site and worked for a total of fifteen days carefully excavating a cluster of nine rooms in Building XII (see figure 9, page 27) and screening each bucket of dirt from the room fills.

Gramly published the results of that field work in the 1998 New Mexico edition of <u>The Amateur Archaeologist</u>, Volume 5, in which he reported that:

> Architecturally, there were few surprises. The rooms were rectangular prisms with walls of adobe bricks covered with adobe plaster. The plaster was unadorned except, in a few cases when it had been painted a uniform red. A few circular holes or concavities at chest height in two rooms suggested the presence of looms or, perhaps, ventilators. The room floors were compacted earth, smoothed so well in places that they shone. Very shallow hearth basins containing wood ash and charcoal were noted in the corners of Rooms A and G. Room A also contained an unslipped jar or pot buried beneath the floor (the rim was flush with it) for storage. But apart from a line of post holes in Room B and artifacts scattered about floors that were buried in place due to room collapse, our nine rooms were essentially featureless. Apparently the occupation had not endured long enough for extensive alterations to the rooms to have taken place. The sole exception was Room G, which had a blocked trapezoidal doorway low down at the center of its western wall.

Barton Wright

Originally the doorway must have led out onto the plaza, and the weakness of this outer wall necessitated the erection of a stone-faced buttressing wall. The space between the doorway and buttress was filled with dirt and refuse, and the door itself was sealed with bricks.

The crews soon discovered that the roomblock in which they were working was at least two stories high. Gramly noted:

> Entrance to the lower tier of rooms was likely by ladders standing in roof-holes. Some rooms in the upper tier, however, may have had horizontal doors in their walls, for we unearthed two thresholds (Room B and surface of Room I). These rectangular blocks of igneous rock, 30-35 cm wide, had been polished to satin smoothness by the passing of countless thousands of human feet.

The artifacts recovered by Gramly, too numerous to mention here, included pottery bowls and ollas, comals, metates, manos, fetishes, stone axes, arrowheads, drills, beads, gaming pieces, bone flutes and whistles, lightning stones, pot and floor polishers, quartz crystals, and bone awls.

About 11 grams of charred maize (corn) cobs that were taken from Room A and submitted for radiocarbon analysis dated the room at about 1445. Gramly's report states:

> Thus, in all probability we can say that our large, C-shaped building at the northern edge of San Lazaro Pueblo was occupied in the fifteenth century, well before the arrival of Spanish explorers and clerics. Our finds represent New Mexico puebloan culture in full flower and without any admixture of foreign elements.

The field schools also concluded what we had discovered elsewhere in our excavations, that the ceramics at San Lazaro were ably formed but almost carelessly decorated. Gramly reported:

> The decorative motifs had become clichés; certainly motifs had become so abstract that they could hardly convey meaning to uninitiated (first-time) viewers. It seems to me that the prehistoric San Lazaro culture was inward-looking and perhaps at peace with itself as well as its neighbors. The trade in turquoise from nearby quarries provided avenues of contact with outsiders for part of San Lazaro's population, but the bulk of the inhabitants, especially women, children, and aged adults, likely received no such stimuli. Their culture continued to tread its time-worn paths.

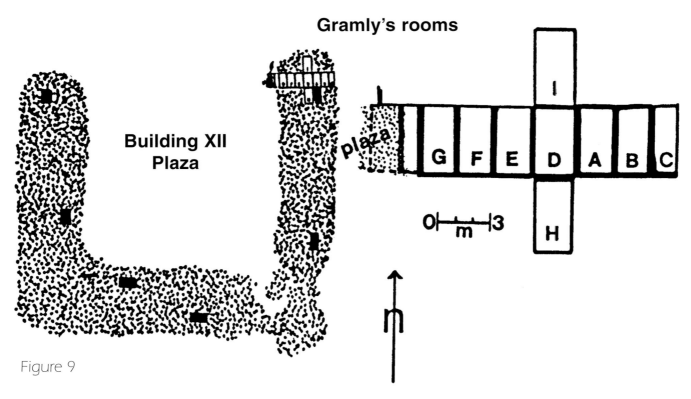

Figure 9

Gramly's report included this diagram, which show where his ASAA members worked in Building XII during the 1997-98 summer field schools. The small black rectangles indicate the rooms Nelson excavated in 1912.

MOUNTAIN LION

This non-gender, sandstone fetish was photographed to look as if it were walking through the grass near Room H in Building XII, where it was recovered. One must wonder what ancient ritualistic duties it performed.

Plate 14

The drawing by Carole Gardner shows the fetish as well as an outline of its actual size.

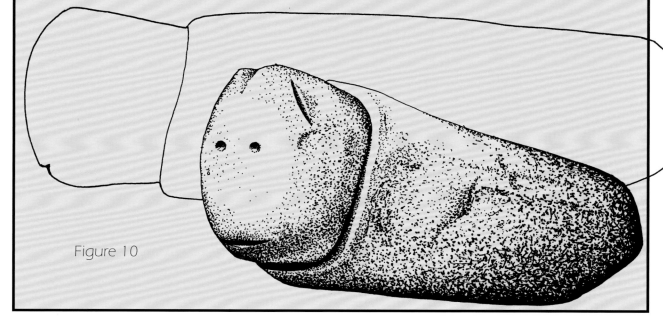

Figure 10

Gramly's archaeological philosophy, which is slanted toward education for everyone who is interested in the subject, is presented in a simple, logical manner, devoid of jargon. His approach may be unique in today's largely computer-oriented world of professional archaeology. The Purpose Statement of his society says that the ASAA:

> ... is founded upon a premise that the past may be studied by anyone—no matter what their educational background, age, sex, or ethnic origin. Archaeology is a social science with many branches and callings. Excavation and report writing are the usual activities one associates with archaeologists, but collecting and curating are just as necessary. There is scope within the discipline for diverse tastes and backgrounds. Some persons are more adept at field work, while others are more at home in libraries and museum exhibits. The practitioners of archaeology are a diverse lot; such diversity gives strength and should be welcomed.

The report on the ASAA's two-summer field work (300 man-days) completed at San Lazaro on June 17, 1998, was in publication for all of its members to read by November of the same year. We admire and applaud the timeliness of Gramly's report.

Subsequent to the departure of the field school, all nine of the rooms were backfilled to protect them from the devastation of nature and livestock.

GRAMLY'S ANTLER ROOM

Figure 11

Don Eckler examines a cache of mule deer antlers that Gramly's crew discovered in the fill of Room E in Building XII. None of the 25 antlers were on the floor of the room, so they may have been on the roof or in a room above, but fell in when the ceiling collapsed. The count is a conservative estimate because antlers closer to the surface were so deteriorated that an accurate count was impossible. Gramly feels that they were trophies that attested to the hunting prowess of the inhabitants. Since three white quartz lightning stones and two badger paws were found among the mass of antlers, we feel that the collection could have been part of an altar of some kind. This is the only situation where we have found more than one antler in close proximity to another.

GRAMLY'S MEDICINE CACHE

Gramly's crew discovered this cluster of artifacts near the west wall of Room D in Building XII, about 5 feet from where the cache of deer antlers was found in the adjacent room. Because of this discovery, Gramly believes that the antlers, the various lightning stones in Rooms D and E, and all the other ritually significant artifacts in Room D belonged to the same upper level room, which collapsed into D and E. He said, "The room may have had an altar and was a depository for important magical devices."

Object 1, a broken bowl with an interior design of a macaw; 2, an overturned bowl fragment with twenty-one lumps of yellow ocher inside; 3, a complete square bowl containing yellow ocher powder (see plate 85, page 132); 4, a small jar with butterfly handles (see plate 17 and figure 13, page 33); 5, a bone scraper

Figure 12

Plate 15

Item 6 in the photo to the right is shown here in detail. It is composed of fifty-seven objects that include ten quartz crystals, twenty-three fluorite crystals, seven gray and brown pebbles, six white quartz pebbles, a hematite cylinder, a large bone scraper, and a 4,500-year-old archaic projectile that must have been picked up someplace and brought home. It is not unusual for archaic artifacts, such as this, to be found in association with ritual objects. Originally the assemblage probably was contained in some kind of pouch.

GRAMLY'S ROOMS

Plate 16

Looking east toward the Arroyo del Chorro and the boulders beyond, this view shows rooms F, E, D, and A (front to back) in Building XII that were excavated by the field schools of the ASAA under the direction of Michael Gramly. The two middle rooms contained the deer antler cache and the ritual objects.

The green and red plants in the foreground are perennials called Curly Dock. Their leaves, which are rich in vitamins A and C, don't taste half bad if you are very hungry.

BUTTTERFLY JAR

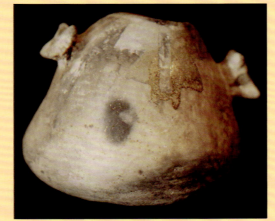

Plate 17

Certainly this jar must have been part of an altar assemblage. We call it the "butterfly jar" because of the shape of the two handles, which are unique to our knowledge. It was recovered near the west wall of Room D in Building XII by a member of the ASAA field school.

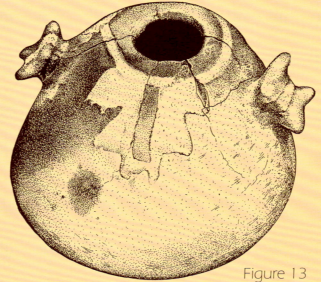

Val Waldorf drew the butterfly jar in actual size.

Figure 13

Gramly and his crew uncovered these three large cooking vessels and one polychrome olla in Building XII. The olla is about 14 inches wide.

Plate 18

MEDICINE BUNDLE

Plate 19

The thirty-three pieces of medicine pictured here, which were found lying together near the floor of Room 2 in Building I, had probably been in a leather pouch, as indicated by the eleven pebbles in the top row that show extensive bag wear. In the second row are seven quartz crystals and a large calcite crystal, all of which are deeply worn on at least one face.

The two lightning stones in the center have been rubbed together so much that a deep groove has been worn into the one on the right. In the fourth row on the left are two pieces of shaped volcanic pumice. The fetish in the center has been percussion flaked from a basalt biface.

On the right is a skunk skull that archaeologist Eric Blinman describes as follows:

> Mephitis mephitis maxilla and mandible that were modified in antiquity. The cranial vault was broken off, removing the upper nasal bones, orbits, mandibular condyles, and the back of the skull; a deep cut mark is preserved on the upper exterior surface of the left jugal. The vertical rami of the mandible were cut and broken off, with cut marks preserved on the lower rear margin of the left horizontal ramus and on the upper broken margin of the juncture between the horizontal and vertical rami of the right mandible. Polish is present along the lower margins of both mandibles, greatest to the rear and decreasing anteriorly until there is no evidence of polish in the area of the symphysis. The polish extends upward on the exterior surfaces of the horizontal rami to approximately the alveolar portion of the bone. Polish on the interior surfaces of the rami is not as well developed as that on the exterior, and it is not discernable anterior to the middle of the rear molar. Interior polish also extends only up to the two rearmost projections of the palate and the rear stub of the right jugal. No other surfaces or broken edges of the vault show distinct polish. Skull and jaw were articulated at discovery, and the pattern of polish suggests that skin was in place over the top of the head and the chin. It is possible that the head was part of the skin pouch that contained some or all of the clustered artifacts.
> Whew! (author's note)

The concretions in the bottom row are typical of those found in nearly all of the medicine bundles excavated at San Lazaro. The largest one, a piece of brown siltstone with brown and gray chert layers, was probably used as a pestle. High points on all the concretions show noticeable polish.

CHRISTMAS TREE

Plate 20

The two objects pictured here must certainly be added to the list of mysterious artifacts recovered by our excavations in Building I. The slate arrowhead on the left, which is 8 1/2 inches high, 6 inches wide, and 1/4-inch thick, was made by scratching deep grooves on both sides of the top in order to break it off of a larger piece of stone. The edge was ground all around until it was smooth and velvety to the touch, and red ocher was applied to both faces after they were polished.

The "Christmas tree," which was made from a 5/8-inch-thick piece of schist, has a back side that looks just like the front. It was found standing upright in the corner of a room. The limonite paint that divides each face has a central line that appears to have been made with the use of a straight edge. Both of these objects may be unique.

PERISHABLE OBJECTS

It is always unusual to find artifacts that have been made from perishable materials in ruins that are constantly exposed to the elements, so we feel fortunate to have discovered as many as we have. My guess is that if you could have taken a stroll through the plazas and looked up on the roofs of various roomblocks at San Lazaro during the height of their occupation, you would have seen thousands of biodegradable objects. Undoubtedly you would have noticed bows and arrows, planting sticks, feathers of all kinds, woven garments and blankets, various food stuffs such as corn, beans, and squash, wooden ritual objects, ladders, ropes, children's toys, rabbit nets and snares, and a constellation of other objects that the inhabitants used in their daily activities. By contrast, the artifacts pictured in this book were made mostly from very durable materials such as bone, clay and rock. Unfortunately, they represent a very small part of the overall picture.

POTTERY HUMAN FIGURINES
Life-size drawings by Carole Gardner depict prehistoric clay figurines that were found in Building I.

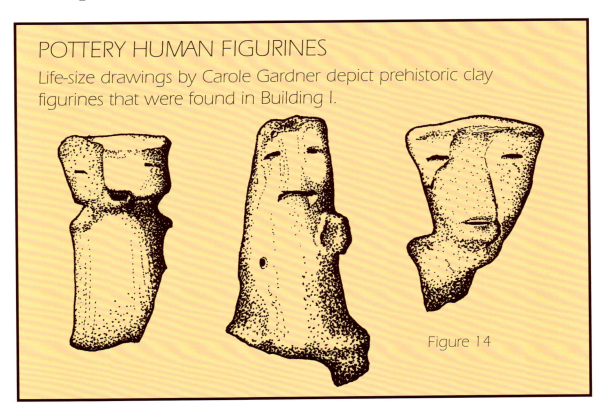

Figure 14

MASKS

Plate 21

Watercolor painting by James Asher

On a warm August afternoon in 1992, I was working alone in Room 4 of Building I. It was nice to be out in the fresh air enjoying the solitude of only myself and the ancient rooms that surrounded me. There was a lure about the place that seemed to beckon me to come and uncover, then study and tell the world. Those chronic thoughts were a compelling tonic to

my spirit, so I welcomed them, of course. It was a good day when all seemed right with the world.

My work was taking me slowly across the floor of an average-looking room, moving north to south. We had not found anything noteworthy in the room fill, just lots of sandy dirt, roots, several large pieces of ceramic bowls, an abundance of smaller pot sherds, lithics, small pieces of bone, and rocks of varying sizes—the usual stuff.

And then, as if a switch had been turned on, pieces of medicine began to appear under my trowel—lots of concretions bunched together, marine fossils, quartz crystals, arrowheads that had been ground into shape instead of being flaked, painted rock circles, a flaked stone animal fetish, bone tubes, shell pendants, stone objects that had been flaked to look like the claws of some giant animal—more than sixty objects in all. Most of them were within an arm's reach of a small door in the southeastern corner of the room that led into Room 2. Somehow I sensed that these discoveries were only a prelude to something much more important.

The numerous ravens that inhabit the area were in the air as usual. Some of them nest in the larger piñon trees around the edge of the pueblo. I am sure they regarded me as an intruder only to be tolerated as they flew by on their way to wherever it was they were going. But this day was about to turn in a different direction and lead me on a journey of discovery that would last many months. And Mr. Raven would be part of it.

As my excavation took me closer to the south wall, my trowel moved the dirt away from two large, white plaster objects. They were something that I had not seen before, and candor compels me to admit that I did not know what they were, or even what they were made of, although they looked like the sides of case masks. Several colors were visible, and the objects

Carole Gardner

were not dissimilar from what I knew the Hopi had worn over their heads in some of their ceremonies.

I sat and stared at these partially uncovered objects for a few moments, but was mentally distracted by the yelling and screaming of a raven that had deliberately singled me out. He was circling about 30 feet overhead, going round and round, yelling all the while. Although he struck me as only an amusing distraction, he would not leave, so I wondered why he didn't just go on about his business, whatever that was.

Although it was not evident to me at the time, in days to come I would look back at the incident and wonder if the raven might have been trying to tell me something. The rapid chain of events, prompted initially by the discovery of numerous items of medicine and then by the exposure of the white things, caused me to pause.

These unusual objects were too important for me to remove alone. I laughed at the raven and at myself as I walked the 100 feet to my car phone to call John Ware, an archaeologist, whom I asked to come quickly and bring help, more cameras, and lots of suggestions.

It was over an hour before he arrived, but the wait was worth it. He brought with him two more archaeologists, George Gummerman and Doug Schwartz, director of the School of American Research in Santa Fe. After a close inspection of the artifacts, we decided that archaeologist Eric Blinman should be the one to actually recover the masks. The next day he arrived with Ware and Edmund Ladd, an archaeologist who was the curator of ethnology at the Laboratory of Anthropology in Santa Fe and an expert on Southwestern Indian cultures. I had dealt with these men for a few years and knew them to be the best for what I needed.

Ladd, now deceased, was a good-looking Zuni Indian with long hair, a quiet demeanor, and a sly, winking wit. Everyone liked Ladd, so when he asked to have a minute alone with the objects to perform a blessing ceremony, we waited at the car. The usual ceremony was quick and simple, consisting only of spreading cornmeal on the objects and saying a few words. It didn't take long, so he soon waved us over.

There was only a wisp of wind as we were climbing down the ladder into the room. Everyone began to talk at once because this was something exciting. As plans were being discussed and organized behind me, I looked at the partially uncovered masks. Where was the cornmeal that Ladd had scattered? Then I saw it, a neat pile on the top of the wall about 4 feet above the masks. By this time, Ladd was smiling at me because he knew he had been found out. He said, "You know, Forrest, I'm a full blood Zuni Indian, but I am also a scientist. I didn't want to contaminate the masks." We both laughed as he turned to finish a conversation with Schwartz and Blinman.

Almost immediately a small dust devil appeared out of nowhere, and with a slight swooshing sound, swirled most of the cornmeal away, much of it falling on the masks. At first I couldn't believe what I had seen and wondered if there were silent agents at work here. I didn't have the nerve to tell Ladd what had happened, although maybe he knew. In any event, I have remembered that little incident for a long time.

After Blinman finished excavating the masks and associated objects that were close to them, everything was transported to the Office of Archaeological Studies, where he worked as deputy director, and the entire assemblage was analyzed by him and his co-workers. Blinman stated:

> The masks were resting on the floor along the south wall of the room. Their faces were turned toward the southeast, and the snout of the western mask rested against the wall. The masks are similar in form and decoration,

MASKS

Plate 22

The two plaster masks in situ were facing the wall with the snouts protruding out the other side, so they couldn't be seen from this angle. They were painted with five colors—green, black, red, gray, and white. In an attempt to find the sources of the colors, we enlisted the aid of four scientists from Lakehead University, Thunder Bay, Ontario. We certainly appreciate the efforts of Philip Fralick, Stephen Kissin, Joe Stewart, and Neil Weir. The different local pigment sources that were analyzed include red and gray clays, a piece of sandstone with copper traces that was found on the floor with the masks, some shales, also from the room floor, and coal deposits that outcrop a few miles west of the pueblo near Madrid.

The scientists who published the results of their investigation in <u>The Journal of Archaeological Science</u> (2000) reported that the green color came from oxidized copper minerals such as malachite, azurite, and chrysocolla, which are found locally. The red color came from an iron-bearing mineral, probably hematite. In some cases, the red paint was mixed with finely crushed selenite to lighten its color. It is possible that plant juices were used as binding agents for the red paint.

The black color could have been made from either charcoal or carbonaceous shale, probably the former. The locally found gray clay was surprisingly ruled out as a source for the gray color on the masks. Instead, it was found to be a mixture of amber-tinted gypsum, a small amount of carbonaceous material, and white gypsum.

The masks were constructed by first building a cylinder of bulrush that was formed around a wooden hoop foundation. Blinman described the process:

> The bulrush elements were held together by open twining with thin two-ply cordage (probably yucca). The projecting bulrush elements were pulled together into a dome at the crown and were trimmed, with the cut ends apparently on the interior of the dome. The irregular exterior surface of the crown was covered by matted fibers, probably yucca. The armature had decayed completely suggesting that weak wood, such as cottonwood root, had been used. Plaster was applied over the armatures in batches, starting with the bulrush cylinder. Details such as the ears and nostrils were modeled, and finish coats of plaster were applied. Paint was then applied to the plaster surfaces, completing the construction.

Carole Gardner

with only slight differences in construction details and overall appearance. The most significant difference is a reversal in one aspect of the color scheme. Faces and snouts of the masks had been crushed during the ceiling collapse, but although they were cracked, the vaults had remained largely intact. Neither vault had completely filled with earth, and reinforcing armatures had rotted, leaving the masks in extremely fragile condition.

The masks are full-headed, helmet-style coverings that rested on top of the wearer's head rather than on the shoulders. The eye holes may or may not have been open. If the eyes were open, it is likely that the wearer would have been able to see out of only one eye at a time, swiveling his head within the mask to do so. The mouth area was closed, with no facilities for either speaking or blowing smoke through the mouth.

Blinman concluded that the animal represented by the mask was clearly zoomorphic, with a projecting snout, modeled nostrils, lips and teeth. The nostrils were large cavities in the red-painted, blunt front of the snouts (see plate 28, page 49), reminiscent of their placement in carnivores. The lips were parted, and exposed between them were closely spaced, vertical reeds representing teeth. The ears were reduced to only shallow slots or depressions. One mask had two small holes drilled through the plaster, one at the apex of the crown and one at the base of the collar. Although these holes could have helped secure attachments, no trace of either ties or attached material has survived.

Specific suggestions have indicated that the masks represented either bear or badger. The snouts were relatively broad and short, more similar to those of badger than bear, and the white stripes on the neck, chin, and top of the snout were similar to those of badger. Further circumstantial evidence was provided by the presence of at least four badger paws in the ceremonial room suite. Because both bear and badger are important figures in medicine society rituals, the interpretation of the assemblage as a whole would be the same regardless of the animal identification.

Another category of ritual objects found in Room 4 was five wooden staffs, all of which may have supported plaster objects that were stored with the ceremonial items. Two of the staffs were lying on the floor near the south wall beside six wooden ears of corn. Although the staffs were rotted beyond recovery, it was determined that originally at least one of them probably had a softball-sized, red plaster object attached to one end.

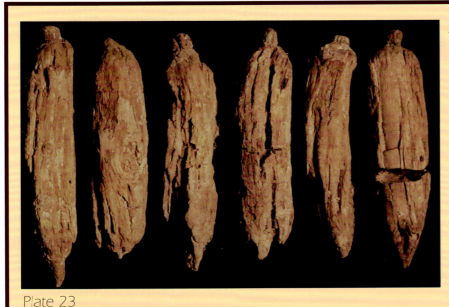

Plate 23

Although most of the organic materials in Room 4 had decayed, so were not recoverable, these six corn effigies carved from juniper are an exception. They were discovered along the south wall stacked side by side immediately west of the masks. When first discovered, they were covered with yellow pigment that either remained on the floor of the room or fell away from the decaying surfaces as the wood dried. The longest ear is 7 inches.

Three other 35-inch wooden staffs were propped against the wall in the southeast corner of the room near the door where they held a red plaster head (see plate 31, page 58).

Blinman thinks the abandonment of the ceremonial assemblage was within a decade or two of 1500.

RITUAL OBJECTS

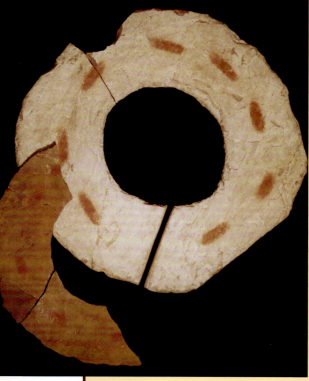

Plate 24

The parts of two stone rings pictured here were found near the east wall of Room 4 in the approximate positions shown. The smaller one, which was slightly thicker than 1/8 inch, was chipped from tabular lavender sandstone. If it had been complete, its outside diameter would have been about 12 inches, with a 6-inch hole chipped in the center. Both faces of the ring had been painted yellow, then red dashes had been added on each face, probably with a finger.

The larger stone ring had an outer diameter of 14 1/2 inches, was 5/16-inch thick, and had a center hole that was about 6 1/2 inches wide. A 3/16-inch-wide groove had been cut through, and both sides had been ground and smoothed. A buff-colored clay pigment had been applied over the entire surface of the stone including the edges. Over the buff background, eight red dashes had been painted on both sides of the ring.

The Tewa elders said that such stone rings are altar pieces that serve as supports for medicine bowls. The groove in the ring had been intentionally cut to allow any spilled medicine to escape.

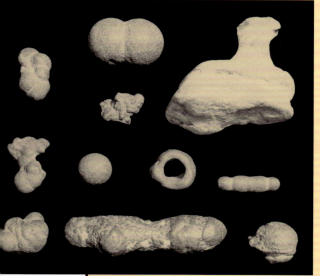

Figure 15

These concretions that were found in Room 4 near the masks were part of the ceremonial assemblage. The large concretion in the top right corner is sandstone, and the other ten are iron. None of their surfaces appear to have been altered by man. The rod-shaped concretion was found within the hollow cylindrical concretion, which might suggest some fertility ritual or sexual connotation. The Tewa elders said the concretions represented animals invoked by the medicine people to help in the curing.

MORE RITUAL OBJECTS

All of the artifacts pictured here are part of the ceremonial mask assemblage discovered bunched together on the floor in Room 4. The five stone artifacts in the top row were described by Blinman:

> All five are carefully shaped by flaking or grinding into elongate forms. Although one is an obsidian biface with a broken tip, the flaking patterns of the others are not consistent with patterns that would be followed to produce an arrow point, spear point, or knife. Instead, flaking and grinding were used to sculpt four of the five into these specific forms. Two of the pieces are obsidian (probably Jemez), two are chert (probably Pedernal), and one is basalt. All exhibit the rounding and polishing of edges, ridges, and surfaces associated with pouch wear. One of the obsidian pieces is strongly reminiscent of a claw, and the entire cluster is interpreted as a set of claw effigies.

In the second row are three bifaces with edges that are abraded and dull, and ridges that are ground flat. The third object is a marine brachiopod fossil. The fourth is a four-legged animal effigy that was flaked from flint, probably alibates.

In the third row are a small pottery gaming piece, two marine shell pendants drilled for suspension, a small basalt arrow point, and, in the middle, a pink travertine pendant with three holes drilled for suspension.

In the bottom row are three quartz crystals, an unmodified botryoidal chalcedony nodule, two bone tubes, and three modified bone tools. The Tewa elders suggested that the rock crystals were used to "look into and do the medicine," and that the bone tubes "were used like straws to prepare the medicine in the medicine bowls."

Plate 25

His conclusion is based on multiple lines of evidence, none of which is conclusive by itself, but together they constitute a strong circumstantial argument. The dating of the entire roomblock is relevant to the dating of both the ceremonial roomsuite and the ceremonial assemblage.

Eric Blinman works on plaster fragments of objects in a room adjacent to and south of where the masks were recovered. Whatever they had once been, they were crushed beyond recovery or even recognition. They may have been hanging from the ceiling or placed on the floor, where they were destroyed by the room's collapse. The only recognizable artifact that was recovered here was a small turquoise disc with holes drilled in each end.

Plate 26

Pottery types on the surface in the vicinity of Building I date from 1400 to 1520, as do the San Lazaro Polychrome vessels recovered within this small study area, indicators that the occupation of the ceremonial roomsuite was within this broad range of time.

Ten tree ring samples were taken from Room 6, which is also within the ceremonial assemblage area. Some of the samples were unusable, some were duplicates, and all were of ponderosa pine. The dates obtained were 1321, 1441, 1455 and 1456. The earliest date is probably the result of reuse of timbers from an earlier construction or the use of old wood. The later date cluster (1455 and 1456) includes two probable cutting dates and indicates construction or final remodeling likely occurred in the mid-1450s.

SNOUT DETAILS

After the fragile pieces of selenite had been reassembled, the snout of one of the masks looked like this. Is it that of a badger, as the archaeologists believe, or of a bear, as the Tewa-Hopi elders have stated?

Plate 27

Plate 28

Inside the upper part of the snouts, impressions were left when the reed teeth disintegrated and disappeared. Note the horizontal line that was made by the twisted string that had held the teeth in place.

Because of the fragile nature and relative importance of the objects, our work progressed very slowly. When the masks first appeared, nearly all of the paint on their surfaces was intact, but as time passed, the swirling wind blew much of the paint away. This is the second selenite plaster mask in situ after the first one had been removed. The bottom portion of the snout can be seen to the left.

Plate 29

An archaeomagnetic dating sample was taken from a hearth in Room 3. (An archaeomagnetic date is based on the location of one of the earth's magnetic poles at the time of the last hot fire in an earthen feature such as a hearth). The date obtained was post 1420, but a date after 1450 also is plausible. The accuracy of archaeomagnetic dating leaves a lot to be desired.

Radiocarbon (C-14) dating was done on a bone from the badger paw that had been hung from a staff near the masks. The result indicated a 50 percent probability that the paw date was earlier than 1473.

Although there always is a degree of uncertainty within the individual dating techniques, the combination of these processes suggests a date for the use and abandonment of the ceremonial assemblage at between 1450 and 1520.

Historic documents may narrow the dates even more. Pedro de Castañeda, who was Coronado's most reliable diarist, reported in 1541 that some of the Galisteo Basin pueblos had been abandoned for more than sixteen years. One of these pueblos is thought to have been San Lazaro, because Castañeda reported he saw large catapult balls on the ground (see plate 186), which suggested to him, without careful inspection, that the pueblo had been under siege and abandoned. Since San Lazaro is the only pueblo ruin in the Galisteo Basin that has a great abundance of large, round, sandstone concretions in the vicinity, which might have resembled catapult balls, it must be the site to which he referred. That scenario would put the initial abandonment of the pueblo at about 1525, which concurs with Blinman's opinion that the pueblo was first abandoned between 1500 and 1525.

In the fall of 1992, soon after the discovery of the ceremonial assemblage, Charmay and I (working through Ladd, Blinman, and Ware) invited eight Tewa-Hopi elders from Hano on First Mesa to visit the San Lazaro ruins and view the ceremonial assemblage, including the masks. It was generally agreed that the Tewa-Hopi people were the closest living relatives of those who finally abandoned San Lazaro during the revolt against the Spanish in 1680.

On April 28, 1993, the Bear Clan chief arrived with a delegation of clan elders for a round of formal consultations. The delegation consisted of six elders, including three of the oldest who spoke only Tewa, with the Bear Clan chief providing translation. The younger men spoke to us in English.

On the morning of the 29th, we toured San Lazaro with Blinman, Ware, Ladd, Tim Maxwell, Director of the Office of Archaeological Studies and, of course, the elders. For lunch, we had buffalo burgers cooked on a grill using for fuel charcoal from an abandoned room in the pueblo. The elders thought it was great and expressed that sentiment to us.

In the afternoon, we returned to Santa Fe to view the assemblage and discuss their interpretation of the artifacts. The non-plaster objects in the assemblage were laid out as they had been found on the room floor, and, to the extent that their condition would allow, portions of the masks had been reconstructed on sand beds. The elders asked to view the artifacts in private without interaction with outsiders.

After the viewing, a three-hour discussion was recorded on audio cassette and video tape. An explicit goal of the consulting party was to use this consultation as an opportunity for cultural revival, and to reaffirm the knowledge of their connections to the Rio Grande Valley. The Bear Clan chief started the discussion with an opening statement:

> We have with us members of the original clans that moved from the Rio Grande area to Hopiland—the Bear Clan, the Corn Clan, the Tobacco Clan, and the Cloud Clan. We toured the ruins of San Lazaro. We think it may be

Carole Gardner

MASKS' LOCATION

This figure shows where the ceremonial mask assemblage was discovered in Building I.

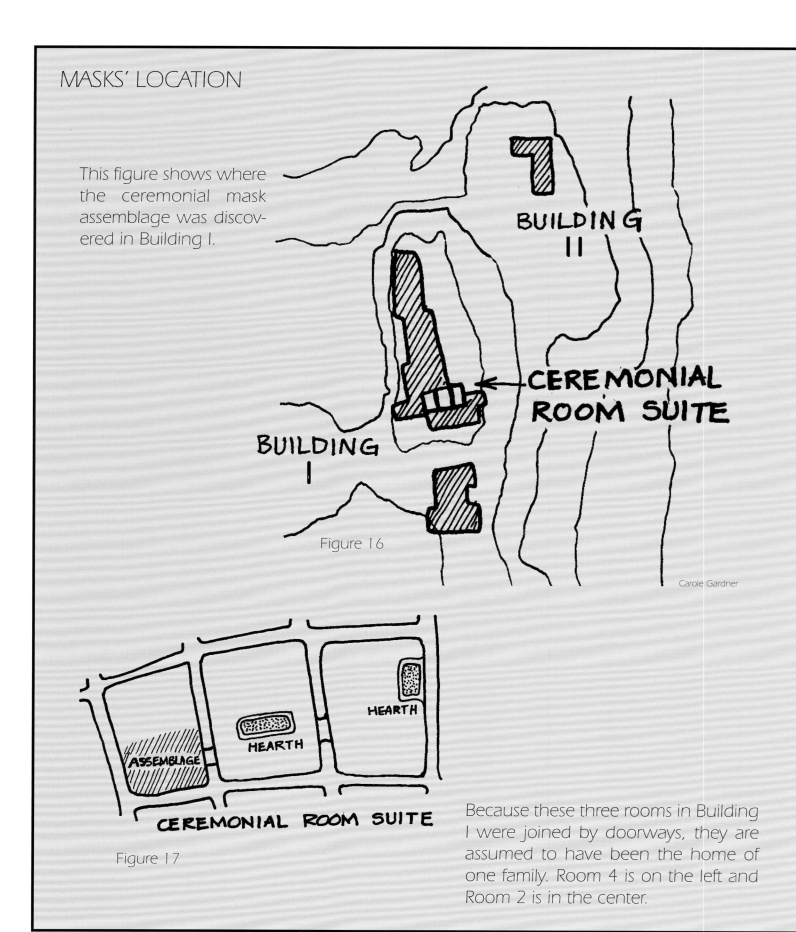

Figure 16

Carole Gardner

Figure 17

Because these three rooms in Building I were joined by doorways, they are assumed to have been the home of one family. Room 4 is on the left and Room 2 is in the center.

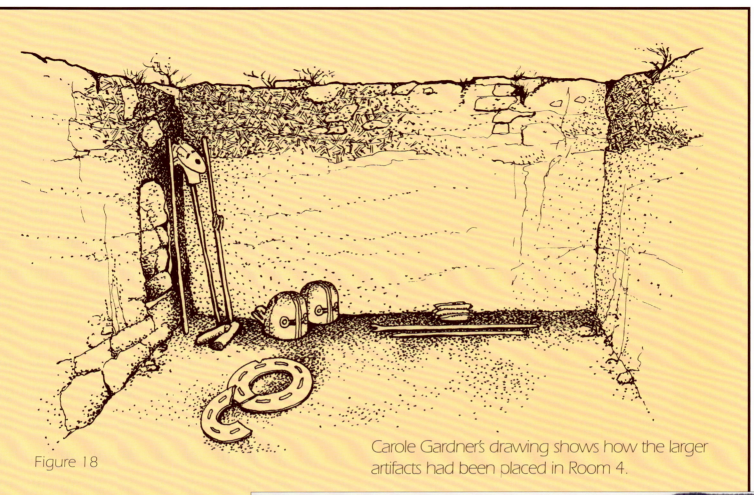

Figure 18

Carole Gardner's drawing shows how the larger artifacts had been placed in Room 4.

Elmer Guerri, who is an amateur archaeologist and collector, took this photo, which faces north across about half of Building I, several years after the mask assemblage was recovered from Room 4 (the bottom room in the center). Other ceremonial material was found in the adjacent rooms.

Plate 30

related to part of our legends, and we are repiecing the history back together. At certain times of the year, we go to the history of our migrations before we got to Hopi-land. And part of the history recites, perhaps, the name of the village and we are taking it under advisement and consideration. We're asking questions to more specifically identify the village. We're impressed with what we saw and have identified a few things that we use today and in the past—the artifacts and some of the things that we saw in the ruins. The village itself is in a location where one of the names in our history coincides with that particular name.

And then, each elder speaking in turn related his impression about the visit to the pueblo site that morning. They were unanimous in their opinion that San Lazaro was an ancestral Tewa site, and that the site was perhaps ancestral to Tsewaddi, the last known Tewa village on the Rio Grande. It was from Tsewaddi that the Tewa were invited to move to Hopi to protect the inhabitants from surrounding aggressive tribes who were stealing their crops and taking their children. A member of the Bear Clan said:

> It just gives me a good feeling. I felt like I was at home. This is the feeling I got from being there because of what I learned and what we have in our history, our legends that we still hold to as what we call ourselves, the Tewa-Hopi. For that reason, I strongly believe that this is one of the areas that we eventually moved from.

Another of the elders related part of an oral tradition that describes an ancestral village located at a place where the canyon narrows down, a place where antelope were driven and trapped. In their legends, the place is called Tonkaweele, which means literally, "place where antelope are trapped." He believes that

San Lazaro may be Tonkaweele because of its location near the mouth of a canyon (the Arroyo del Chorro emerges from a narrow canyon just a mile south of San Lazaro).

After discussing their impressions of the site, the elders turned to talking about the ceremonial assemblage viewed earlier that afternoon. They were unanimous in concluding that the material was associated with the Bear Medicine Society and consisted of a medicine man's ceremonial paraphernalia. They said the Tewa have always had medicine "groups," and the bear group is by far the most powerful. These Tewa bears go from village to village performing their medicine "chores." Because one of the informants claimed to have witnessed a bear curing ceremony, he was certain that the material from San Lazaro is related to bear medicine.

Most of the objects composing the assemblage consist of things that are arranged on a medicine society altar. Altars, which include sand paintings and numerous feathers, are set up for a particular curing ceremony and then taken down after the ceremony is completed. Looking at the distribution of artifacts in the reconstruction drawing, the elders agreed that the room was a storage area for such curing paraphernalia. They said the masks, which depict bears, were worn by medicine men during the curing ceremony. Typically masks of this type are made over a basket foundation, but the meaning of specific decorative motifs, such as the open circles and central line, would be known only by someone who had been initiated into a particular medicine society. In response to a specific question, the elders stated that bear masks were no longer used in curing ceremonies.

We asked why the assemblage might have been left behind. Did the society simply die out? They thought that was unlikely, since the Bear Society is very much alive and functioning today. The elders speculated that the   ritual   materials   were   left   behind   because

MANOS

These two nearly exhausted manos were recovered from the floor just a few inches east of where the masks were resting. All five colors on the masks also were found embedded in the rough surfaces of the manos. Although both had been used on slab metates, some areas of gray or tan appear to have been made by grinding heated selenite to make plaster. Blinman thinks, "The residue pattern is consistent with the manos' use as a passive abraders or palettes rather than as hand stones. In other words, the pigment source material was rubbed on the mano surfaces rather than having been ground by moving the manos over the pigments on a metate."

Figure 19

something bad happened—a drought, famine, or disease—and that the people left with no intention of returning.

Because the masks and the related objects might have been associated with something bad that happened in the past, the elders were not interested in having the objects returned to them. Their only suggestion was that the material be treated with respect.

It has been widely reported in archaeological writings that kachina dance or other ritual masks probably did not exist in the Southwest in prehistoric times, despite the fact that they are seen as figures painted on pottery vessels, on the walls in kivas, and in rock art. Dr. Fred Dockstader, who believed that it would be very unlikely to find kachina masks in prehistoric ruins, wrote in 1985: ". . . although many villages were abandoned in ancient times and in a few that desertion seems to have been precipitous, it may be said with some certainty that masks would have been the last thing the inhabitants would have left behind."

If those assumptions are true, then the unique assemblages we recovered at San Lazaro are exceptions. Our recovery of the two masks (see plate 22, page 42), the effigy head (see next page), and the two effigy faces (see plate 33, page 60) are important in that they are the only known prehistoric gypsum plaster artifacts that have been found in the American Southwest.

As far as we know, the kachina cult is still active in nearly all contemporary pueblos today, with possible exceptions of the Tiwa communities of Picuris and Taos. Fundamental to the cult belief is the idea that the kachina spirits speak to both the pueblo people and their gods. In ceremonies, the human dancers wearing kachina masks impersonate the spirits and transmit prayers to the special gods that control fertility, health, rain, and other important things.

DOG BONE RASP

Although bone flutes, flageolets, and whistles are common at San Lazaro in both the historic and prehistoric components, this rasp is the only other type of musical instrument that has been recovered so far. Made from the 6-inch-long femur (leg bone) of an Anasazi dog, it was found on the floor of a room on the north end of Building I.

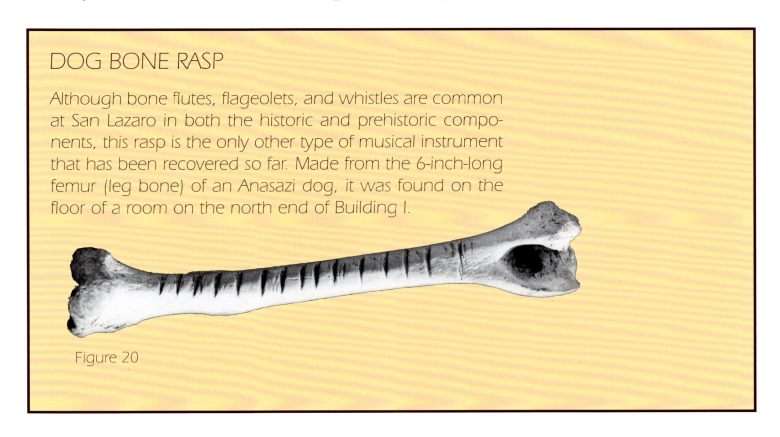

Figure 20

RED HEAD

Plate 31

The red selenite plaster head, shown here in situ resting on a 35-inch wooden staff, appeared 2 feet east of the masks. (see figure 18, page 53). Two similar staffs were standing nearby, one of which had the left paw of a badger tied to it. Three bone tubes, cut from turkey bones (tibiotarus), which were discovered in the vicinity, probably were originally tied to the other staff. This figure, about three-fourths the size of a human head, had been crushed by rocks falling from the upper wall of the room. Its face, which had suffered water damage, featured a circular mouth and long, slit-type eyes shaped from pot sherds placed in the plaster. Areas of the face had been painted red with a black overlay to indicate hair, but it had no nose. Eric Blinman described the head construction like this:

> The armature for the head was supported by cross bars tied to the support staff. Matted fibrous material, possibly yucca fiber, was built up over the wooden elements. The neck portion was wrapped with a small mat constructed of sedges held together with open twining using thread, probably yucca, as the weft. Thread was wrapped over the cylinder of matting of the neck and sparsely over the core of the head to

hold the materials in place. Plaster was then applied over the surface, and the limited features (eyes, mouth and chin) were modeled in place. Pigments were then applied to the surface, but were not mixed into the surface, and they were probably applied with a mastic binder.

A radiocarbon sampling taken from materials within the head produced a date of about 1445. This is one of five known plaster objects that have been recovered in the prehistoric Southwest, all of which came from a small area of rooms in Building I. At least two additional plaster artifacts were discovered in the same vicinity, but they were in such poor condition that their shapes or uses could not be determined. These objects add another new and important dimension to our knowledge of the past, where a void has existed for so many years.

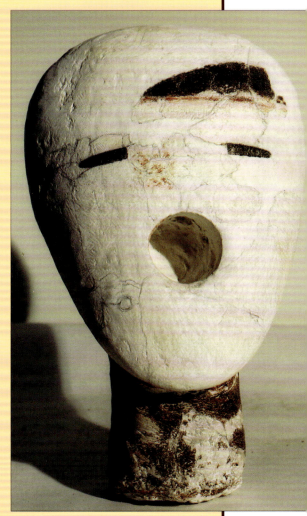

Plate 32

Artist Rob Turner made this reproduction of the plaster red head (see plate 31, page 58), which shows the shape and some of the details that were on the original head.

Figure 21

The impressions made in the plaster inside the neck of the red head were formed by sedges, probably a bundle tied with a twisted string, as indicated by the vertical line.

PLASTER FACE

Plate 33

Figure 22

Carole Gardner

This is one of two plaster face masks that were resting on the floor of Room 26 in Building I. Evidently they had been hanging from a ceiling beam, and both had fallen together. When I first discovered the jumbled mass of painted plaster, I called Ware and Blinman to hurry out to the site and untangle the puzzle for me. At first we didn't know what we were looking at because the top mask had fallen face down on the other, so both were pretty badly broken. Individual fragments of each face were removed one at a time and placed in separate containers. Finally, after all the pieces had been collected, we took them to the Office of Archaeological Studies where Roland and Martha Mace "jig-sawed" the pieces back together. It was an arduous and time-consuming task. Although I am sure both masks had been molded three-dimensionally to look like human faces, this one was reconstructed on a small mound of sand that was quite flat. Black mineral paint covers the face, while red paint can be seen around both the inside of the mouth and the outside perimeter of the face. White vertical lines run down from the bottom lip and disappear under the chin, although the chin itself is gray.

The drawing of this plaster face is a realistic interpretation of what it probably looked like when new. Holes on either side at the hair line that are 10 inches apart may have been used to attach the object to someone's head or to a carrying staff, since the goggle eyes are solid and cannot be seen through. Charmay thinks the drilled holes were used to attach hair or a headdress to the face to make it look more realistic. Nothing like this has been seen before in the Southwest.

STIRRUP POTS

Although stirrup pots are rare in Southwestern archaeology, Nels Nelson recovered a few whole pieces while working in the Galisteo Basin in the early 1900s, and A. V. Kidder found a few fragments at Pecos Pueblo. These life-size drawings by Carole Gardner depict the two fragments we excavated in Building I. Both have glaze decorations on the handles.

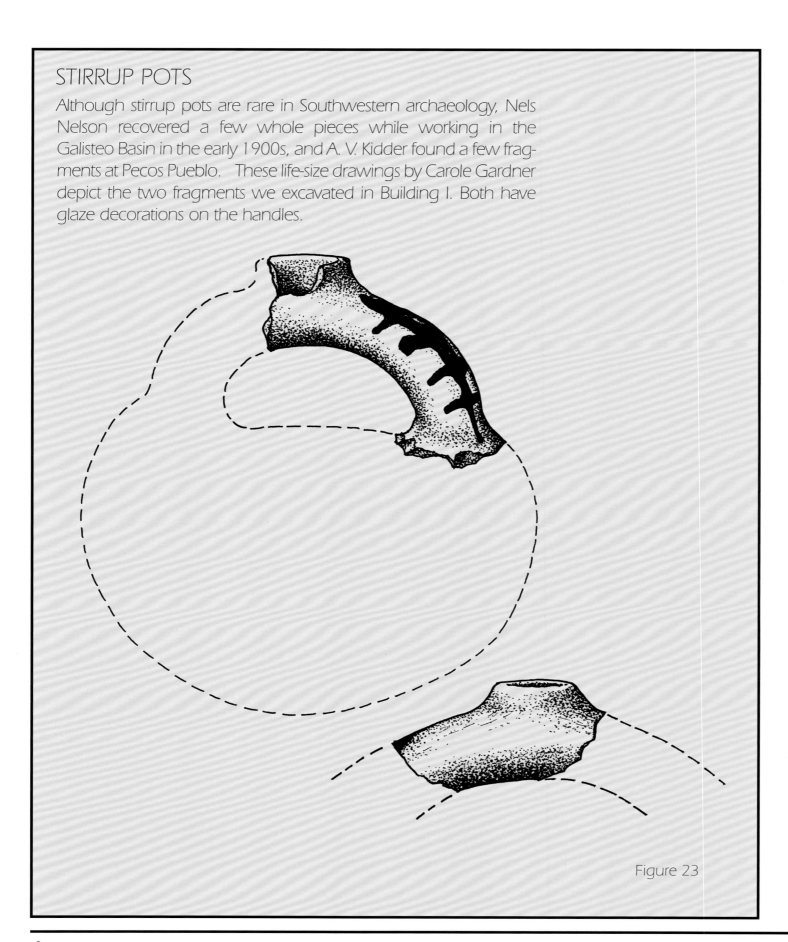

Figure 23

STONE SHELL PIPE

This pipe was carved from a piece of talc to imitate a Strombus shell. The idea of carving stone "shells" probably originated as a result of trade with natives from Central America, who brought large conchs into the Southwest. Such shells could be used as sounding horns after the pointed tip of the shell had been ground off to expose the orifice. This pipe was recovered from a room in Building VI that had been occupied from about 1330 to 1400.

Plate 34

Figure 24

These life-size drawings show two sides of the pipe. Instead of drilling into each end of the stone to produce one continuous air line, intermediate holes were drilled in the bottom to join with shallow holes on each end. A groove scratched between the two inner holes, which produced one continuous line through which smoke could pass, necessitated the use of a second stone to cover the groove, which probably was attached with cordage. Although the pipe does not appear to have been smoked, there is fire damage on its surface. Life size drawings by Carole Gardner.

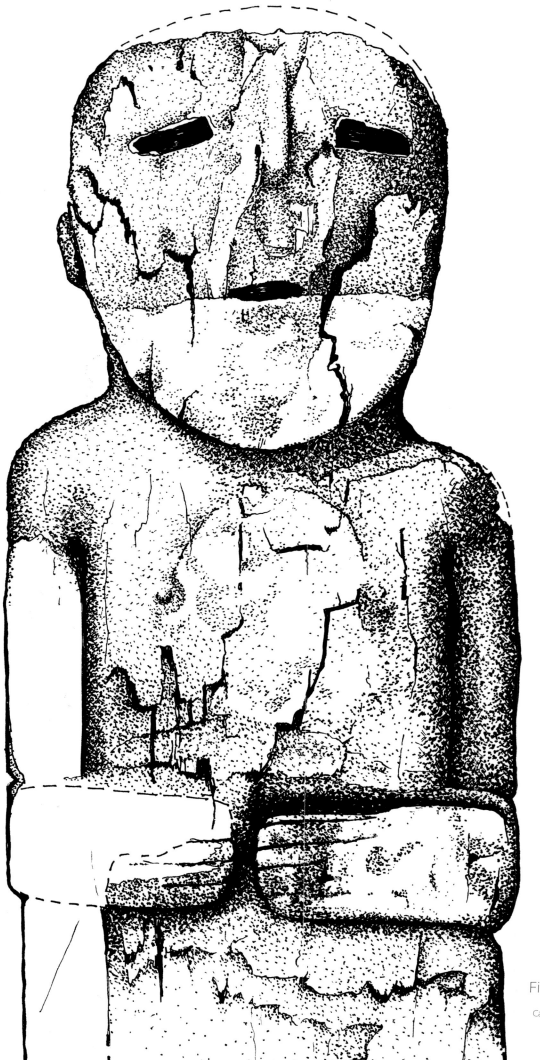

Figure 25

Carole Gardner

WOODEN EFFIGY

Sometime in the early occupation of Building I, this wooden effigy was placed on the floor in the northwest corner of a 4-foot-deep room we call Room 26. In 1994, when we were excavating the room, surprisingly we uncovered the head of the figure. At first, we had no idea what we had found. However, when its nose and left eye appeared, we knew it was something special requiring the expertise of a specialist like Eric Blinman.

The figure was standing in damp, sandy soil where it likely had been for many decades, perhaps centuries. Although wood in the ground can become saturated with water rather quickly, it is difficult for it to dry out under those conditions. Since the effigy's head was soaked, we quickly covered it, making it as airtight as possible, and ran to call Blinman.

As the face and body of the effigy began to emerge under Blinman's trowel, we thought its right eye was missing (It was two days later, in our lab, that conservator Keith Bakker removed the mud that had hidden that eye.)

A later inspection revealed that the figure had obsidian eyes, an obsidian mouth, three-dimensional ears, an elongated nose up between its eyes, nipples, and arms with articulated fingers across the chest. White selenite plaster covered the area from the mouth to the bottom of the chin. It had pink pigment on the chest that became red as it moved down the sides.

This powerful sentinel had been carefully placed, facing wide-eyed across an empty room, assigned to its final post. Diagonally across the room was a door merely 15 inches high and 11 inches wide, which curiously had been sealed from the adjacent room and plastered over so well that its construction went almost unnoticed.

The wooden lady was carefully removed and placed in a plastic container lined with paper towels over aluminum foil. Her box elder body was 10 1/2 inches tall, but it may have been an inch or so taller when she was new. She was 4 1/2 inches wide at the shoulder and 3 inches deep. It was obvious that she had suffered too long from slow deterioration and the harsh treatment of time.

Two conservators who worked trying to stabilize the wood gave a sad diagnosis, stating that she could not be saved, and when she dried, nothing would remain but a mound of brown powder and three flakes of obsidian. Fortunately, our treatment proved them wrong. We placed a lid on the container, wrapped it tightly in a black plastic bag, and stored it in our refrigerator for more than three years. When the wooden lady finally emerged from her long, cold sleep, she was dry and amazingly intact. We were happy that we had thwarted the failure that had been patiently waiting

Because of her extremely fragile condition, even now, nine years after we found the lady, we still have not seen her back. A radiocarbon date places her age at 563 years, give or take a few. She looks pretty good for a lady with that many birthdays.

Both conservators told us that we were at least a hundred years too late recovering this beautiful wooden woman, which emphasizes once again the urgency to excavate archaeological sites. The well-worn slogans "Save the past for the future," and "If it doesn't have to be dug, don't dig it," are not intelligent options when important information is being lost as perishable objects lie rotting in the ground. Principle is always a convenient excuse for ignoring logic.

Plate 35

This is the wooden lady as we discovered her, standing in the corner of a room. We can only wonder what forces were at play while she was being carved and dressed in white and pink. We feel awed and respectful in the presence of this object and thirst to know more about it.

Plate 36

A close-up view of the wooden figure's head, taken by an archaeologist, shows the face of a very sensitive woman. To me, she seems only too human, but looks tired and sad, and although her 563 years have wrinkled her face and rotted her body, she still has the same determined, resolute expression with which she was born. We have become much attached to this person, despite the intrusion of the photographer's impersonal, scientific scale that rudely mars one side of her face.

STONE EFFIGY

Figure 26

In 1912, Nels Nelson assigned several men to excavate at San Lazaro under his supervision. They eventually uncovered and reported on about sixty rooms. A survey of the recovered artifacts and related data, now held and mostly hidden in the American Museum of Natural History in New York, reveals that the work must have been both arduous and generally unrewarding.

Then one day a worker discovered something very important. On the east wall of Room 1 in Building VI, a stone figure was uncovered. The only record of the event, other than a casual mention in the field notes, is a photograph taken at the time of the discovery that reveals a human effigy that had been carefully pecked and ground out of a beige, grainy stone. Its eyes, nose, mouth, and hands are in relief. Even the fingers are articulated. The sculptor may have been spiritually motivated, judging by the quality of his art and the amount of time that must have been allocated to the job. Reddish-brown pigment covers the entire figure, both front and back, except for the middle third of the face. The top of the head comes to a rounded point, where someone placed the number 1289. Somehow that seems out of place to us, even irreverent.

The photograph and Nelson's field notes also tell something about life in the pueblo. In the same room with the effigy his men discovered eleven metates, twenty-four mullers (manos), two cooking "slabs," a bird bone flute, ten bone tools, and other assorted objects.

Neg. No. 15950, photo N. C. Nelson, Courtesy Department of Library Services, American Museum of Natural History

Evidently this stone effigy was a very powerful and important deity to at least a few and, perhaps, to a whole culture. One thing is for sure; it is a most beautiful, compelling, and haunting object, standing 15 inches high, 4 inches wide, and 2 inches deep. Over 150 years after it was made, a Spanish soldier wrote home to say he was surprised that there were so many idols at San Lazaro.

Neg. No. 5170 (photo by J. Beckett). Courtesy Department of Library Services, American Museum of Natural History

Plate 37

HEARTHS

Every woman seems to have a different idea about what a stove should look like, an idea substantiated by these five photos that show a few of the different styles of hearths that have been uncovered at San Lazaro. Some hearths have rocks, called fire dogs, standing vertically around their outside edges, upon which a flagstone comal (grill) was placed for cooking. Hearths may be round, square, rectangular, deep, shallow, large, or small. They may be located adjacent to a wall or in the middle of a room. A few hearths that appear to have been built only for the purpose of heating the room usually are deep, small, and have had fires so hot that they cooked the dirt around the edges, turning it bright hues of brown, orange or red.

Since only about one in six rooms shows evidence of having had a hearth, we assume that most fires were built only for the purpose of cooking, and so were located on the roof. It is common to find burned fire dogs and comals in the fill of collapsed rooms. This reminds me of a saying I learned as a Boy Scout: "The white man builds a big fire and freezes; the Indian builds a small fire and stays warm."

My guess is that after the inhabitants had been living at San Lazaro for a hundred years or so, they may have had to search as far as a mile away to find firewood, so standing trees would have had to have been felled, which must have been a labor-intensive act to accomplish with a stone axe. For that reason, they probably were very frugal in their use of wood.

Carole Gardner

Plate 38

An unusual hearth was discovered mid-wall in a room in Building I that was 6 feet wide and 15 1/2 feet long. A rectangular flagstone comal that once rested on the firedogs, which include the mano on the left, was found collapsed into the ashes that covered the floor of the fire pit, the base of which is a metate that had been laid into the floor. One end of the metate can be seen just inside the stone that outlines the hearth at left. Another outlining stone (parallel to the trowel) is also a mano.

Our guess is that originally this feature was a bin in which corn was ground in preparation for cooking. To create the hearth, the metate was probably just left in place, and the three fire dogs and a comal were added to complete the remodeling.

Plate 39

Why there are two hearths side by side in this room is a mystery to us. Each of them contained a layer of ashes and, although the bottom dirt has been discolored by fires, the outlining stones do not appear to have been burned, nor is there much evidence of smoke on the walls. Perhaps they were originally mealing or storage bins that later were converted to hearths.

This hearth is located in the southwest corner of a room in Building I. Near the north wall a metate still rests on the floor where it was used for grinding corn.

Plate 40

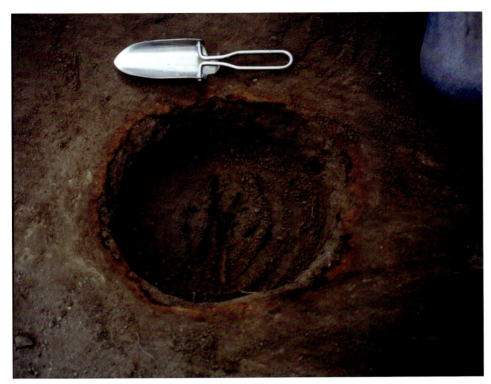

Plate 41

Carved into the floor of a room in Building I is this round, 9-inch-deep hearth, which was probably used only to heat the room. No burned bone residue or other evidence of foodstuff was found in the ashes. The red discoloration of dirt around the edge is a testament to the presence of hot fires that burned over a prolonged period of time.

Portions of Building I were constructed over rooms that had been built about 200 years earlier. This hearth was discovered in one of the older rooms, which is located below and to the east of the room where the mask assemblage was uncovered. The hearth is deeper (16 inches) than it is wide, which makes it different from most fire pits, and the red, cooked dirt around the edges is evidence that it got very hot. The fires probably heated the floor for a foot or so around the hearth, which would keep the room warm for several hours after the fire subsided.

Archaeomagnetic testing of the hearth indicated that the last fire burned in it sometime after 1225 and before 1275, dates that are substantiated by the dominance of Galisteo Black-on-white pottery in the sub-floor deposits in the adjacent mask roomsuite.

Plate 42

COMAL

Plate 43

This flagstone griddle rests on three fire dogs over a hearth in Building I. Black smoke smudges can still be seen on its surface, although about 550 years have elapsed since an ancestral puebloan woman last used it to cook for her family. The horizontal white groove through the smudge was made when someone used the rough surface of the comal to abrade a hard object, like the blade of a stone axe. The long rock at the extreme right in the photograph marks one end of the hearth in which the ashes of many fires are still present.

TRASH MIDDENS

A number of trash middens scattered among the buildings at San Lazaro were used mostly as places to discard broken and unwanted objects that might otherwise interfere with good housekeeping. Pot sherds, bones, and stone tools make up the majority of artifacts that were deposited in the mounds, some of which, in time, rose to a height of 4 feet. That is not to imply that refuse was not randomly tossed as someone's whim might dictate. Any ruined room seemed to be a fair depository for garbage and litter, and every room we have excavated has had hundreds, and sometimes thousands, of pottery sherds mixed in with other debris as the room collapsed.

THRESHOLD

Plate 44

A prehistoric stone threshold, which was found in Building I, is made of an igneous stone called latite. Most of the roomblocks are made of this rock that is formed by volcanic action. It is found in great abundance in the high, vertical bluffs up the Arroyo del Chorro two miles or so from the pueblo. On cold days, when the south-facing cliffs are rapidly heated by the sun, large stones such as this one sometimes pop off the wall, making a loud sound similar to that of a rifle shot. Old-timers say that the stones can fly as far as 10 feet out as they cascade below. They are then washed downstream in the flash floods that come with sudden summer thunderstorms.

It is easy to see by the lack of wear that the ends of this threshold were placed in the lower sides of a door wall leaving the center portion to be walked on by those entering and departing the room. The heavy wear in the center laps over the edges both front and back, leaving us to wonder how many bare feet it took to produce that wear, and for how many generations. The threshold measures 2 feet, 3 inches by 9 inches by 3 inches.

CLAY MINE

In 1912, Nels Nelson took this photo from the bottom of the Arroyo del Chorro, facing southwest to the entrance of the clay mine. Buildings I and II are on top of the rounded hill in the center. Note the lack of trees and other foliage.
Neg. No. 27799, Courtesy Department Library Services, American Museum of Natural History.

Figure 27

Plate 45

Mimicking Nelson's photo made ninety years earlier, this one serves as a metaphor for life in the high desert. The cholla in the foreground dares to threaten a closer view as ominous clouds of a thunderstorm gather above the horizon. Meanwhile, the beautiful landscape of the pueblo entices the imaginative mind. Mother Nature around San Lazaro in ancient times would have been both rewarding and punishing, as she both provided and then took away.

Plate 46

The 4-foot by 6-foot entrance to the clay mine opens up inside to reveal an area larger than an average bedroom, which is probably what this space was used for at one time or another. It might have been a good place to hide during violent weather or enemy raids. Local history claims that several hundred years ago, ancient human mummies were found inside, closely huddled together.

Black soot covers the walls and ceiling of the mine, and a giant pack rat's nest occupies the entire back wall. Corn cobs can be seen in the nest, which encourages us to think the pueblo was occupied when the first pack rat moved in. A 9-inch chimney, which had been excavated through more than 8 feet of sandstone, can be seen at one o'clock to the entrance. Large chunks of clay that have fallen from the ceiling in recent years now partially block the door. At left in the photo is the entrance to a small rock shelter with white painted walls (see plate 47, next page).

ROCK SHELTER

Plate 47

The small rock shelter adjacent to the clay mine looked like this before it was excavated and the wall was restored. The large rocks in the foreground fell from the ceiling in prehistoric times, collapsing the wall that protected the entrance.

Plate 48

The interior of the rock shelter also had been smudged with black soot before a layer of adobe mud was applied to the walls, which were then whitewashed with a thick clay slip. Although pack rats and other small animals were using this room as a dwelling, it was relatively clean. Over the years, ceiling doidle and blow-in debris had covered the floor to a thickness of 2 feet or more, but when Richard Blake and I removed that layer, a beautifully manicured adobe floor was revealed.

In this photo, a metate and mano rest against the north wall, and a round, 4-inch-deep hearth can be seen in the center of the room. Several grapefruit-size balls of yellow and red ocher were discovered just inside the entrance, along with five peach seeds, a few pottery sherds, and some lithics.

ROCK SHELTER & CLAY MINE

Plate 49

After we excavated the rock shelter and swept the floor clean, I restored the wall using dry clay and sand as mortar between the rocks. The reason I didn't use wet adobe, as the original builders had done, is because it was a long way down to the creek to get water, and a hard climb getting back up the hill to the shelter. Forty years ago I might have done it as they had, so the wall would stand for a few hundred years. Unfortunately, Charmay is not much at carrying heavy rocks, so we suspect she would have made a lousy Anasazi housewife.

Carole Gardner

PIPES

Plate 50

Of the sixty-five pipes that have been recovered at San Lazaro, fifty-eight show signs of having been smoked. Many still have burned tobacco in their bowls. Three are made of compressed volcanic ash, one is catlinite, one is sandstone, and the remaining sixty are made of fired clay. Twenty-three of the pipes are decorated in some manner. Nicotiana (tobacco) seeds were found in flotation samples taken from Room 2 in Building I. The pipe in the top left of this photo is 2 1/2 inches long.

Carole Gardner

Plate 51

When we found this deeply incised pottery pipe, which is 2 1/2 inches long, it was lying beside a hearth on the floor of a room in Building I. Because it was encrusted with a heavy calcium deposit that largely obliterated its design, we soaked it in a mild solution of muriatic acid. When the liquid stopped fizzing, the pipe appeared as new.

Plate 52

Burned tobacco can be seen in the bowl of this pipe, which is 3 1/4 inches long and carved from a piece of compressed volcanic ash. Two other pipes made of this same material have been found in our excavations.

THE BATHTUB

About 100 feet south of Building I is an architectural feature we call "the bathtub." This small, man-made reservoir chiseled out of solid rock is located on the sloping, lower end of a large outcropping of Galisteo sandstone. Three feeder canals, seen as dark lines in the photo below, which faces north, direct rain and melted snow into the reservoir.

Figure 28

In 1989, Turney, who made a study of this feature, reported:

> The north-center of the reservoir bottom has a round, possible mortar hole 1.4 feet in diameter that is quite visible. The reservoir shape is roughly a parallelogram with nearly vertical

walls. It appears the excavation may have been done in several stages. The builders may have constructed the large mortar hole first, found that it collected water nicely, then enlarged the volume and added the collection channels.

Turney estimated the bathtub capacity to be 58 cubic feet, a size that would hold about 440 gallons of water. The drainage area is about 350 square feet, so a 2-inch rain would fill the tub.

The main canal, in the left center of the photo, starts 42 feet above the reservoir and, as water is directed down at a 15-degree angle, it is deflected around a large concretion in the rock before it reaches its destination. The original stone pick marks made by the builders some 800 years ago are still visible in the canal, which averages about 3 inches deep and almost as wide.

A peripheral channel, which is 31 feet long, feeds moisture in from the east (right) side of the drainage, but only the first few feet of it can be seen in this photo. Dr. Charles Lang, who assisted Turney in his analysis, suggested that the sides and bottoms of the canals had been rounded and smoothed by the edge of a mano or similar stone tool. A third, smaller canal (11 feet long) directs water in from the left.

Turney estimated that the construction of the reservoir took three person-days, and that the canals required another ten person-days to engineer, chisel, and smooth, making them ready for use.

Studies show that precipitation in the Galisteo Basin, which has not changed much over the last 800 years, averages about 13.2 inches a year. Based on that average, Turney estimated that 2,515 gallons of water could have been taken from the bathtub annually. A Tewa elder of the Cloud Clan commented on the bathtub, "It was used for drinking. They kept that thing clean, very clean. They didn't let anyone so much as even step on the rocks here. They swept it so clean. The trenches were a lot deeper. You can see they've eroded."

Plate 53

From just up hill above the bathtub and facing south into the arroyo, this view shows two canals entering at the right and the peripheral canal in the shadows at the left. The thin line at the left end of the bathtub is the overflow canal.

In modern times dirt, sand, and leaves are always in the bottom of the tub, which can be dry and hot for weeks at a time when the summer monsoon rains are late. When water washes into the tub in the morning, the next day hundreds of tiny tadpoles will appear. They seem to spend their time chasing each other around and occasionally coming up for air. Several weeks later, if all the water has not evaporated, the tadpoles will be miraculously transformed into cute little land frogs with legs that are long in back and short in front. They have to be on the alert for the small water snakes that must find them juicy. Once mature, the frogs are vulnerable to the many birds, coyotes, raccoons, and other predators that live in the area.

Once in a while, in the winter time, we will find one of the frogs, then weighing almost half a pound (and not cute anymore), hibernating as deep as 3 feet under the ground in a room. Although we have discovered no bones of these creatures, I am sure the Indians must have found them to be delicious roasted over an open fire.

Carole Gardner

BASALT BIRD

In Building II we found a cute flaked basalt bird.

Figure 29

ANOTHER MEDICINE BUNDLE

Plate 54

Apparently this little nine-piece medicine kit originally had been stored in some kind of container, but we were not sure. In any event, all of the components were stacked together in a tight group when we found them on the floor in a corner of Room 3 in Building VI. The large rim sherd at the top of the photo contains a four-legged animal design that is at least confusing. It has two humps on its back like a camel, a tail like a kangaroo, and a head somewhat similar to that of a buffalo. When the bowl was whole, it probably contained additional animal figures and what appears to be a swirl design in the bottom. It is the first bowl that we have recovered at San Lazaro that was made of red clay. It measures 4 inches across, is decorated with a black glaze paint, and dates from about 1330 to 1400. The objects below the sherd are two quartz crystals at the bottom, both of which have been heavily smoothed by rubbing, and a multi-million-year-old ammonite fossil that also is worn on all of its high spots. The five crudely rectangular objects are sherds that have been ground smooth on each edge. Normally we could call them gaming pieces, but because they were an integral part of this bundle, we are sure they served some medicinal or ceremonial purpose.

PACK RAT'S NEST

Plate 55

A messy pack rat's nest is nestled in between two large rocks. The occupant must have a good sense of humor and a special eye for art because many large pieces of prehistoric ollas and bowls have been brought in and strategically placed to decorate his home; hence his name. There appears to be a complete sixteenth-century, black, handled, cooking vessel scattered around in several pieces. As I have been watching this little casa through several rodent generations (almost twenty years), I have had to laugh at how the occupant moves certain large sherds around to facilitate his changing artistic fancy. Maybe his wife has something to do with that. In any event, we respect his life style and never have interfered with what he is doing. I am sure he appreciates us for leaving him alone. Note the stylized macaw effigy painted on the large sherd at right.

Carole Gardner

HEALER BASKETS

A shy friend of mine is the consummate hiker and arrowhead finder. He seems to sense where others have not walked, and he scours the ground like a private detective. Several years ago, he stumbled onto a secluded and almost unnoticeable rock crevice near the pueblo. I had walked past it many times before, but had failed to see the two long, plaited baskets that were concealed within its vault. He carefully examined the baskets without touching them or disturbing the space in which they had rested for five centuries. Eventually they were radiocarbon-dated at 1480 ±25 years.

Although my friend has a natural taste for understatement, as he told me about the find, his inflated smile betrayed him completely. We immediately gathered our trowels, measuring tools, sketch pads, cameras, and a screen and went to investigate this new discovery.

The sandstone shelter was on the outskirts of nowhere. It was small, about a foot above waist-high, and although it was 6 feet wide, it had only a narrow 16-inch vertical opening that did little to betray its existence. I blamed my failure to see the shelter on the large bushes that guarded both sides of the entrance. The throat of the shelter quickly slanted down toward the back about 4 feet away, which made it impossible for our arms to reach the back. It was blotter dry inside, and the only disturbance it had seen over the centuries was the insidious flaking of sand particles that had fallen from the decaying ceiling and walls.

After making copious notes and photographs, we carefully removed the baskets and screened the contents of the shelter only to find that there were no other man-made or man-used objects present. Although both baskets were largely filled with white, powdery sand, it was easy to see the numerous plant materials that also were present. Without wishing to

The two 500-year-old plaited baskets seen here were found in a shallow, dry rock shelter near San Lazaro Pueblo. The longer of the two is 25 1/2 inches. They were packed with at least 114 herbs, roots, stems, and limbs (see plate 57, page 92). Their condition is a little rough considering the lack of decay on the remaining fibers. Perhaps they were in the present state of disrepair when they were placed in the shelter. It is also possible that rodents or bugs could have gnawed on them a little, although there was no visible sign of such current activity.

Plate 56

disturb the perishable contents, we carefully removed the heavy sand from the baskets as best we could and retreated to our camp table near Building I at the pueblo, where we performed adequate housekeeping chores on the baskets and took an inventory.

The baskets are long and narrow, closed at the ends, and almost identical in size. One flap on each basket overlaps the other, which closes the opening and secures the contents. Both baskets have a large, woven knot at each end, and it is probable that straps were

attached to them for transporting, although no such straps were found.

The two baskets with their plant contents intact were taken to the Ethnobotany Lab at the Office of Archaeological Studies in Santa Fe, where they were studied by the very competent Mollie Toll and Pamela McBride, with Eric Blinman as the project director. In their report, Mollie and Pamela stated:

> The Galisteo assemblage clearly represents the working pharmacopoeia (tool bag) of a "healer," rather than the kit of a "medicine man" or shaman. Components consist entirely of plant parts with a variety of chemical constituents of known medical usefulness; completely absent of the charms, widgets, talismans (crystals, concretions, beads, semi-precious stones, owl toes, feathers, odd bits of convoluted wood) that are part of ethnographically or archaeologically known shamanic kits. The only non-plant article in the Galisteo baskets is a flint scraper, which may certainly be a tool for gathering or preparation of the plant materials. Two highly toxic materials (iris root, and possibly jimson weed root) are well-associated with connotations of power and danger; their inclusion earmarks the kit as that of a specialist.

They concluded their report by saying:

> At least six of the taxa (plants) found in the baskets (osha, spruce, corkbark fir, Douglas fir, ponderosa pine, iris) point to non-local, high-elevation sources. Of these, osha and iris favor fairly wet habitats (streamsides above 9000 feet, and open meadows above 7500 feet respectively), while ponderosa pine, spruce, corkbark fir, and Douglas fir are residents of montane conifer forests above 7200-7500 feet.

All of these plants could be gathered in the Sangre de Cristo Mountains, about 17 miles to the north. Silvery scurf pea, on the other hand, grows at a lower elevation than the Galisteo Basin, further extending the gathering range of this kit.

Figure 30

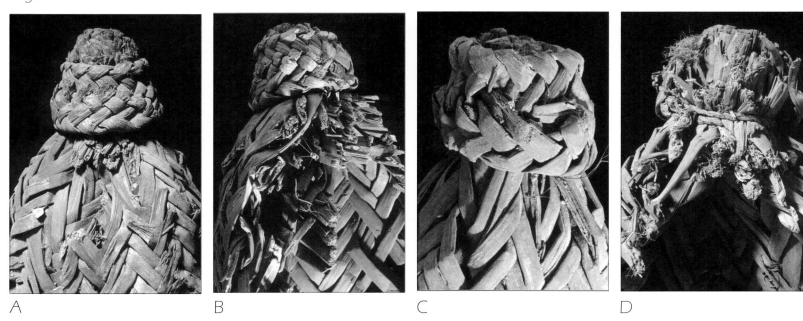

A　　　　　　　　B　　　　　　　　C　　　　　　　　D

Knots A and B, which are on basket 1, are 1 1/2 inches wide, while knots C and D, from basket 2, are slightly larger. The knots on both baskets are similar but not identical. The top side of knot D had been damaged and repaired with two strands of twisted vegetal cordage.

The knots were placed on the baskets for several reasons—for decoration, to prevent the carrying straps from slipping off of the ends of the baskets while they were being carried under the arm, and to secure the basket flaps in the closed position. Entrance into the baskets was gained by prying the flaps apart and reaching in. When the hand was removed, the flaps closed again.

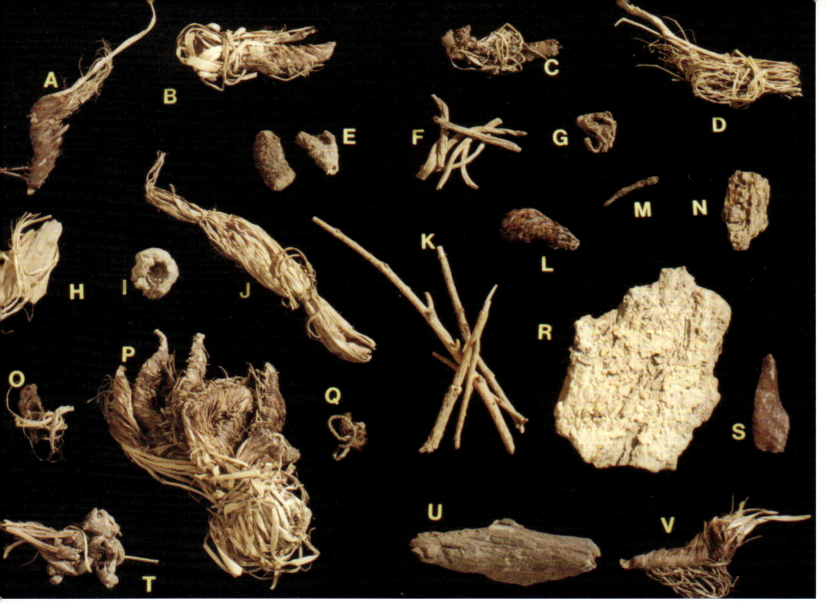

Plate 57

These are some of the contents from both baskets. The number at the end of each description indicates the basket in which the item was found. Identifications were made by Mollie Toll and Pamela McBride.

A. An Iris missouriensis root. This is the only species of iris that is native to the Southwest and found in moist areas above 7500 feet. It can be poisonous. (1)

B. An Iris missouriensis root and leaves tied with a split yucca leaf strip. (1)

C. An unknown root with numerous small, secondary roots tied with a split yucca leaf strip. (2)

D. A bundle of folded stems and leaves of silvery scurf pea tied with a split yucca leaf. The distinctive, pea-like pods of this plant are about 3/8 inch long. The plant can be used as a deodorant when the leaves are moistened in water and applied under the arms or on any other part of the body. (1)

E. Two pieces of osha root, which grows at altitudes up to

11,000 feet and is not seen below 9,000 feet. The most widely used herbal medicine in the Southwest, osha root is effective in treating sore throats, bronchial inflammation, and the early stages of viral infection. (1)

F. Seven fragments of what are probably datura roots. Like iris roots, any part of the datura plant is dangerous stuff, more toxic than healing in the hands of anyone other than an experienced herbalist. Powdered leaves can be smoked and inhaled to effectively relax bronchial spasms or reduce sinus inflammations, or soaked and used as an analgesic or anti-inflammatory agent for sore joints. Roots, however, seem to be restricted in function as a dangerous and powerful narcotic. Ethnographic literature abounds with cautions about this herb's potency, and restricts those who may procure and administer it. (1)

G. A cut root fragment that resembles a Liatris root. (1)

H. A piece of juniper wood tied with a split yucca leaf strip that is very loose, which suggests that some other item was part of this bundle. The identity of this hypothetical second material would be of considerable interest. While the use of juniper wood for fuel, construction, and manufacturing was widespread and well-recorded, we know of no ethnographic record of its medicinal usage. For ceremonial purposes, generally the branches or berries were used, both of which are very resinous. (2)

Barton Wright

I. A piece of root of an undetermined barrel cactus type. (1)

J. A corn husk receptacle that is missing most of its contents. Corn husks are tied together in two places with split yucca leaves. The container has an effective cavity of 4 inches. A piece of datura-type root remains inside along with fragments of hairy dicot leaves. (2)

K. Five corkbark fir twigs. Corkbark fir objects appear frequently in ethnobotanical literature as an important, symbolic talisman. (2)

L. Iris missouriensis root. (1)

M. A spruce twig. Spruce is both specified for many important ceremonies at the pueblos and frequently found as part of the dancers' accessories. (1)

N. A small piece of yellow-brown bark that shows the interlocking puzzle-pieces characteristic of ponderosa pine.

Ponderosa pine bark has been used to dye hides after they have been soaked in water, and the resin has been used as a remedy for skin problems. (2)

O. An unknown root tied with a split yucca leaf strip. (2)

P. Six Iris missouriensis roots and folded leaves tied with a split yucca leaf strip. (2)

Q. An empty tie of two-ply yucca leaf cordage. One end is knotted and both frayed ends are singed. (1)

R. A hunk of bark 5 1/4 inches by 7 1/4 inches, which is the largest single item included in the baskets. The bark is dotted with small globs of resin. Its surface appearance and its thick, spongy texture are identifying characteristics of corkbark fir. (2)

S. A flaked, alibates jasper knife, 3 3/8 inches long, which shows considerable use wear on its concave edge. It was probably used in the gathering or preparation of plant materials. (2)

T. Three entangled root fragments tied with a split yucca leaf strip. (2)

U. A piece of wood from an unknown tree type with green pigments covering one end and a side. (2)

V. Iris missouriensis root with secondary roots and leaf bases. (1)

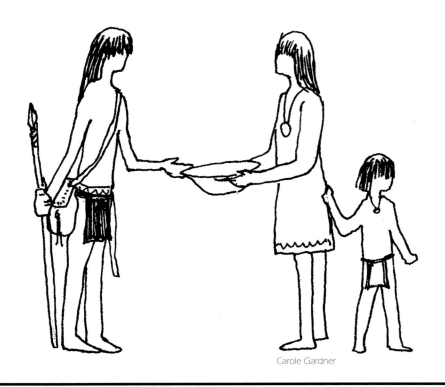

Carole Gardner

SPECIAL MEDICINE

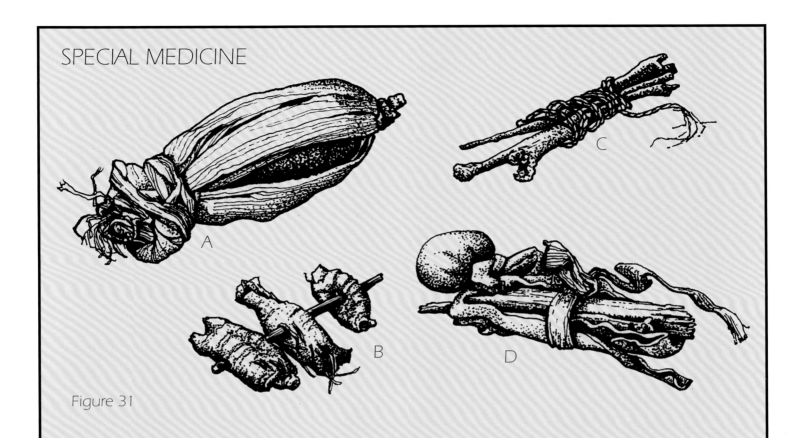

Figure 31

These drawings by Carole Gardner depict four selected medicines from the healer baskets.

A. A "tamale" that is very interesting. A corn husk, with the ear removed, forms the container with the shank joining the husk leaves at the basal end and a tie of husk strips forming the closure at the other end. The contents are a solid mass of clay and coarse quartz sand with some unknown fibers that are visible.

B. Three small pieces of osha (Ligusticum porteri) root skewered on a stick.

C. A bundle of three rhizomatous or stoloniferous stems tied with two-ply, twisted yucca cordage.

D. A bundle of several elements wrapped with a corn husk tie. Small sections of two unknown root types are tied into the bundle, and a small piece of tanned leather, wrapped around a ball of an unidentified powdered substance, also is included. We resisted the temptation to look inside the bag and inspect its contents, thinking it might be fastened with some kind of sacred knot. As these three substances clearly belong together in some context, it would be interesting, indeed, to know their identities.

PIGMENTS GALORE

Plate 58

Paint pigments generally were used to decorate pottery vessels, ceremonial objects, and the human body. Chunks of mineral pigments such as selenite, hematite, azurite, and limonite, which produced colors of white, red, blue, and yellow respectively, were crushed into powder before being mixed with water. Organic paint pigments that usually produced various shades of black were obtained by boiling desert plants such as Rocky Mountain beeweed. In both cases, a liquid paint of thick consistency was most easily controlled when being applied by a brush or fingers.

The stones in the center of this photo are minerals in their original form, while the colors around the outside were recovered in archaeological contexts and reconstituted by us.

BRIGHT COLORS

Plate 59

At San Lazaro Indian paintbrush grows in small clumps, but not in great abundance. Although paintbrush can grow up to 2 feet tall, at San Lazaro it is rarely found taller than 8 inches. Paintbrush acquired its name because the dense blossoms look as though someone dipped them in a bucket of bright red paint. The seeds of this plant usually germinate in the fall and produce plants that bloom the next spring in colors ranging from white to yellow to crimson red and maroon. It is a partial root parasite, so if it is malnourished, it will attach itself as a parasite to the roots of the other plants. Some tribes were known to eat the blossoms and use them as a medicine to treat rheumatism and as a bath rinse to make their hair glossy.

Carole Gardner

CAPITANS

Figure 32

When A. V. Kidder was excavating at Pecos Pueblo starting in 1915, he recovered a number of bowls and sherds that had been painted with designs similar to the one illustrated here. He named this figure Capitan, which is a Spanish word for captain or chief. His Mexican workers, noting its anthropomorphic features and plume-like appendages, thought the name was appropriate.

This 8-inch figure was painted inside a bowl fragment that dates between 1490 and 1515.

Another Capitan figure stretches 17 1/4 inches around the outside of a bowl found in Building VI. The bowl dates from 1330 to 1400.

Figure 33

Figure 34

Mike Brechausen discovered this horned figure painted inside a broken bowl fragment in Building VI. The figure, which is 5 inches long, was painted before 1400.

Art by the author

TURKEY

Plate 60

The first time I visited San Lazaro Pueblo many years ago, I picked up this headless turkey. A friend and I were walking along a small arroyo just south of Building III when I saw it eroding out of a bank. It had been shaped from a piece of pottery, and it appears that the prehistoric craftsman deliberately ground off the turkey's head.

Carole Gardner

BEAD-MAKING KIT

We were cleaning the roof and wall collapse from Room 26 in Building I when we started finding components of a bead-making kit. Many small chunks of turquoise, eventually numbering 368, began showing up in our screens. Some of the pieces were fractured bits 1/8 inch in size that needed a lot of surgery before they would start looking like beads, while others, as wide as 1 inch, were shaped and ground to a high sheen on both sides.

Ninety-two pieces of jet were scattered around and mixed in, as were numerous pieces of slate and catlinite that were patiently waiting their turns to be made into pendants and other forms of jewelry. The story continued to unfold as six 6-inch pieces of slate and other raw materials were uncovered.

Then we found four tanged knife blades and two sandstone bead abraders. The knife blades probably had been hafted to either wood or antler handles so the beadsmith could more easily saw his soft stone into precise bead and pendant shapes and sizes. The knife blade edges were worn flat, a graphic indication of how much they had been used.

The bead abraders were a different story. The beadsmith had applied a thin layer of adobe to the flat surfaces of several small sandstone slabs. Because sandstone is so coarse, he needed a finer surface on which to grind and finish his beads. When the individual square blanks had been cut to the desired thickness and size, a hole was drilled in the center. Then the four corners of each bead were broken off and the beads were strung on vegetal cordage or sinew in lengths of maybe 5 or 6 inches. Knots were tied in each end to hold the beads tight against each other. The jeweler then held one end of the strand against the adobe abrader and rolled the beads at an angle with the other hand, grinding them a little with each roll until

all of them were round and uniform in size. Many Indian bead workers use the same technique today.

Plate 61

Raw material found in the bead-making kit included large pieces of slate and catlinite, as seen in the top of this photo, while 368 fragments of turquoise are shown on the right. On the bottom left are bead blanks and a small group of almost-finished beads. Curiously, only one finished bead was recovered in this cache.

Plate 62

The tools and raw materials that were part of the bead-making kit include, on the right, four stone knives resting on a piece of slate from which beads were to be made. At left is one of the sandstone abraders with adobe applied to the surface. The 5 1/2-inch piece of slate at top right is smoothed on all surfaces. We don't know what that thing was used for.

101

QUAIL EFFIGY JAR

Plate 63

Although this is the only complete effigy jar we have found at San Lazaro, a lot of broken pottery wings and tails have turned up in the trash mounds. Occasionally a vessel that has a body shaped like a bird will be discovered, but it is nearly always an unpainted, black ware cooking jar. This quail-like bowl, which was found in Building I, is 6 1/2 inches wide and 6 3/4 inches long.

BABY JAR

Carole Gardner

Figure 35

Most of the small jars at San Lazaro were made with handles, which probably were more for decoration than anything else. The jar pictured here, which was recovered in Building II, is as wide as it is tall, 1 1/2 inches, and was surely made to be hung because originally it had horizontal handles. When they broke, two small holes were drilled to replace their function. It also has a large, glaze-painted "X" on each side.

ANTS AS ARCHAEOLOGISTS

Carole Gardner

Before my days at San Lazaro, I had thought of the red harvester ants as being the enemy. More than a few times, as a kid, I had been on the wrath-end of what they do best—BITE. The ant's body is about 3/8 of an inch long, so with his feelers sticking out in front and his legs sticking out in back, he can reach just about 1/2-inch overall. Like so many of nature's insect marvels, his small size serves to disguise the wallop of a painfully red, itching, venomous bite that he inflicts, should you enlist his displeasure by approaching too closely to the colony. And worse, when he's aroused, he quickly emits a chemical alarm, and then the whole village of fully armed red ants comes looking for you. That can be formidable, if you hang around.

Once a friend was helping me look for beads in an anthill when she suddenly became terribly excited and started flailing her body wildly while she wiggled her jeans over her hips and down around her ankles. Evidently she was willing to suffer the gross indignities of immodesty rather than the painful chewing of a few rude harvester ants that had found their way up her leg to a soft spot. No apologies were offered by the ants.

The habits of harvester ants (Pogonomyrmex rugosos) that have built their nests in close proximity to the prehistoric buildings at San Lazaro have led Richard Blake and me on a long and exciting path of discovery. Richard, who retired after many years as a solar physicist at Los Alamos National Laboratory, is what I call a severe scientist. His thoughts and focus can be tightly arranged in his method-and-solution-oriented mind. His skills and logic were exactly what I needed, so when I asked him to help me devise a model that might explain the reason why we were finding so many beads and so much turquoise debris in the anthills, it started a chain of discussions, measurements, and mathematical calculations.

Our curiosity was driven by the fact that we have recovered very little finished turquoise jewelry in our excavations but large amounts of waste turquoise in the anthills. It didn't add up. Were the locals making a lot of jewelry and trading it to other tribes? If so, what were the locals getting in exchange?

In our quest for answers, we began collecting beads and bits of turquoise that the ants had deposited on the surface while excavating their underground tunnels and storage chambers. We quickly learned to ignore both anthills that appeared on the tops of structures and those that were more than twelve feet from the outside walls of structures. We found that those hills were not typical in that they contained negligible amounts of turquoise and beads. Instead, we concentrated on the thirty-eight active anthills (called study hills) that were outside a prehistoric building wall, but no farther away than twelve feet. We named that space "ground alpha."

We tried to search each anthill at least once a week in the summer, when the ants were actively both excavating and collecting seeds. We knew that they emerged from their nests at sunrise and foraged until about 11 a.m., when the pebble surface heated to 52 degrees Celsius (125.6 degrees Fahrenheit) and then retreated back underground until it cooled off. For obvious reasons, we tried to hunt in the hills when the ants were underground. Of course, during the cold months, when the ants were content to remain underground to eat the harvest that they had gathered the summer before, no new materials were being brought to the surface.

When we began our search, we wondered if the information we were gathering would be of any use to us. Was anything to be gained by knowing that there are thousands of small bits of turquoise in the anthill gravels (called shields) around the pueblo? And what, if any, was the relationship between the small bits of

turquoise and the travertine disc beads that also were showing up in our study hills? We had a lot to learn.

Hope Merrin, who is an expert on both harvester ants and beads, believes that the raw material for making travertine beads came from the area of the Rio Puerco (between Albuquerque and Santa Fe and a little west near the Rio Jemez). She thinks the beads were made elsewhere and traded into San Lazaro. It was not hard to agree with her, since we have found neither raw travertine nor waste debris that would make us think the beads were being manufactured locally.

Plate 64

Materials recovered from thirty-eight anthills in ground alpha include: in the top row, travertine beads, nuggets of turquoise (unworked and unbroken), black stone beads, and broken turquoise beads. In the center are catlinite beads and turquoise beads. The bottom row consists of unworked fragments of turquoise, broken travertine beads, and flat pieces of turquoise that are worked on one or more surfaces.

We had recovered 328 white, travertine disc beads (sixty-eight of which were broken) from our study hills, so now we were scratching our heads again. Were the local natives trading turquoise jewelry for travertine beads?

Shell beads can easily be confused with those made from travertine because both are the same color and are made of calcium carbonate ($CaCO_3$). However, shell beads are usually whiter, shinier, slightly concave, and of a finer grain than those made of travertine. We have recovered only eight shell disc beads in our anthill research.

After a lot of discussions, we decided to set our research goals high; we hoped to calculate the total amount of beads and turquoise debris that was underground at ground alpha. We assumed that the materials appearing on the surface of an anthill were only a fraction of what was below in the anthill volume.

Our first steps were to identify each of the study hills within ground alpha, mark them on a map, convert their round surface sizes (called their shields) into square feet, and add up the areas. I was happy to let Richard take the lead on that one.

Beads and turquoise bits (called materials) could have been deposited by humans in different strata in various ways. Beads can be lost, placed as offerings, cached, or offered as grave goods. Most of the turquoise bits that have been found were small fragments that look like debris left over from working much larger pieces. Those that originally were deposited on the surface of the ground might have been covered up over the years, only to be brought to the surface again by the ants building new nests. Because most of the materials we have found were buried in the hill gravels, we concluded that the chamber depths extend below the levels of occupational activities.

Carole Gardner

107

Our task, then, was to relate the total amounts of collected materials to the total volume of ground alpha. This was accomplished by using both anthill knowledge supplied by archaeologists and our own observations and assumptions about the distribution of materials over ground alpha. From the literature we learned that for harvester ants the cross-section of an anthill is roughly conical in shape (see figure below), that debris shields on the surface have diameters about equal to the bases of their respective cones (see figure 37, next page), and that the cone's height is generally equal to the shield's diameter. This information was all we needed to compute the total cone volume. Furthermore, the material sampled within a cone is carried to the surface and redeposited onto the shield, where we could measure both the shield volume and its area to obtain the total volume of materials and rocks brought up by the ants while excavating their tunnels and nests. We measured some arbitrarily chosen anthills in ground alpha and obtained a value of 25 for the ratio of total cone volume to excavated volume. Finally, we needed an additional ratio, one that converted the volume of materials to the total ground alpha area. That area ratio was 1050.

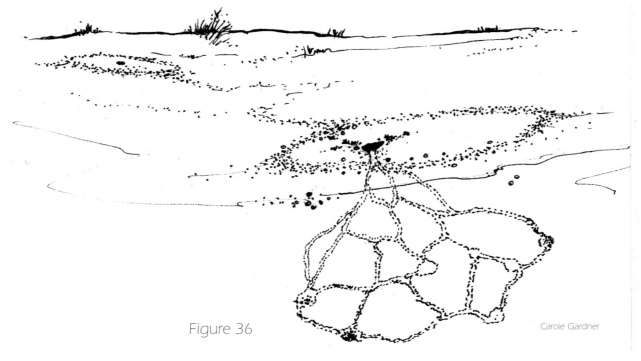

Figure 36

Carole Gardner

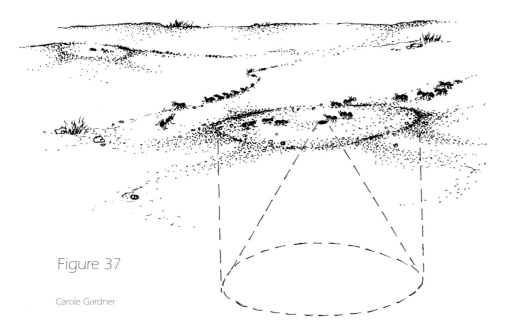

Figure 37

Carole Gardner

The formula for the desired relationship of total materials to total ground alpha volume is just the product (25) x (1050) x (materials collected).

Observed data (materials collected) are as follows:
- 1,787 fractured pieces of turquoise, assumed to have been discarded
- 337 pieces of turquoise that had been worked by man on at least one surface
- 200 broken pieces of turquoise with drill holes present
- 219 nuggets of turquoise, not broken and not altered by man
- 68 broken travertine beads
- 3 broken shell beads
- 2 broken catlinite beads
- 19 black beads
- 260 white travertine beads
- 5 white shell beads
- 18 catlinite beads
- 58 turquoise beads

These figures total 3,074 human-processed materials that have been recovered from the study hills, of which 2,543 are pieces of turquoise (3.62 oz) and 531 (0.607 oz) are beads of all sorts.

The total amount of materials still in ground alpha equals the total of materials recovered from the study hills multiplied by the volume and area ratios. These numbers for materials recovered, multiplied by the grand ratio (25 x 1050) equal 67 million total pieces of turquoise with a weight of 6,000 pounds, and 14 million beads and fragments that weigh 1,000 pounds.

Richard's measurements and calculations are too complex for me to understand, so I decided not to include them here. However, his mathematical formula is so much fun I cannot resist letting everyone see it:

$$TM_{ga} = TM_s \times V_c \times A_{ga}/A_e = TM_s \times 25 \times 1050$$
$$= 67 \text{ million pieces of turquoise } (6{,}000 \text{ pounds})$$
$$= 14 \text{ million beads \& fragments } (1{,}000 \text{ pounds})$$

Carole Gardner

Although in the excavations at Chaco Canyon of features dating from 900 to 1150 more than 100,000 pieces of imported turquoise were uncovered, Richard and I found our numbers to be surprisingly large. We checked and rechecked our calculations, and despite some assumptions in our blueprint, which were impossible to evaluate accurately, we concluded that our figures were representative of what materials remain in ground alpha. Still, we were not satisfied for some gnawing reason, so we went back to the books.

About eleven miles northwest of San Lazaro are the turquoise mines in the Los Cerrillos Hills, the most prominent of which is located at Mt. Chalchihuitl, a name that means blue or turquoise. It is believed that the first date of mining at the site was about 500, and that large quantities of the blue stone were used by both Mayan and Aztec craftsmen. Interestingly, Sydney Ball, an engineer, estimated that 100,000 tons of rock had been removed from the mine before 1540, when the Spanish arrived.

If Ball was right, then our figures would seem logical indeed. San Lazaro is the largest pueblo near the Cerrillos Hills, and, if its prehistoric residents took only 1 percent of that 100,000 tons over a 200-year period, say, from 1300 to 1500, that would be 1,000 tons, or just 27 pounds per day. Our estimate of 3 tons of debris is only 0.3 percent of what they took out as turquoise ore. This is a small percentage of waste, which makes our estimate in ground alpha quite reasonable. I am sure the San Lazaro turquoise miners processed as much of the ore as possible at the mine to lighten the weight of their material for the walk home. That probability is emphasized by the fact that we have found no pieces of turquoise larger than 1 inch that are still in the matrix.

We have concluded that the natives were heavily into the exportation of turquoise to other areas, including Central America. That assumption is based on the fact that we have found very little finished jewelry, but a lot of turquoise scraps. However, in our excavations of prehistoric rooms, there is little evidence that much was received in trade for jewelry or anything else, for that matter. We have recovered thirty-four scraps of shell, the remains of two macaws, and Nancy Bloch found a jadeite bead in an anthill—that's about it. Because of our relatively small sampling of rooms, it is possible that we just have not happened on the right area. However, in Nelson's field notes of work he did in the sixty rooms he excavated in 1912, there is no mention at all of turquoise.

It never will be known how much obsidian, fibrolite, basalt, and other tool-stone might have been taken in trade for jewelry, but my guess is that there was very little because those raw materials were readily available within two days' walk. However, there is plenty of evidence that pottery made at other pueblos was used at San Lazaro. We are not sure what all of this means, and the evidence one way or the other probably will not be significant until much more work has been done. We feel a little like Nelson must have felt; we have done some scratching, but we still itch a lot.

JEWELRY

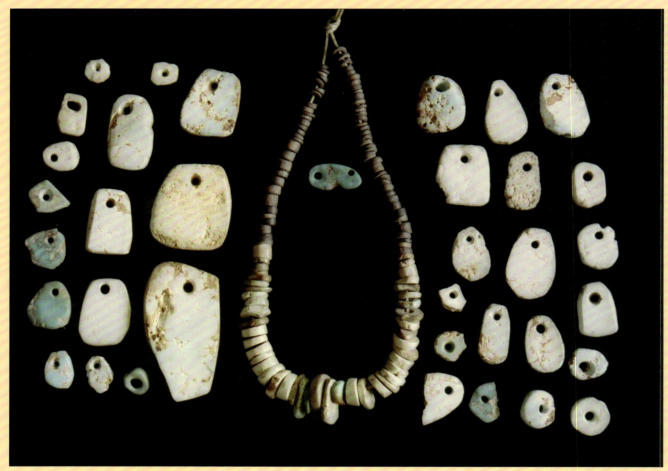

Plate 65

Except for the fifty-eight beads that have been recovered from the anthills, this is all of the turquoise jewelry that we have found at San Lazaro. The necklace in the center was found intact, and although the cordage on which it had been strung had deteriorated, the beads have been restrung in their original sequence. The small disc beads at the top of the necklace are made of black slate, and the forty-two on the bottom are made of turquoise.

Carole Gardner

PENDANTS AND BEADS

Plate 66
The small white arrowhead in the center, which is partially covering a bead made of catlinite, was found in the anthill beside Building III. Note the small fragment of turquoise in the top center of the picture.

Figure 38
These selenite beads and pendants were found in prehistoric rooms.

YET ANOTHER MEDICINE BUNDLE

Plate 67

All of the medicine bundles found at San Lazaro contain highly specialized components, and this one is no exception. The forty-nine pieces shown above were found together on the floor of a room in Building XIII. Eleven of the thirteen quartz crystals in the top left show considerable bag wear. In the top right are twenty calcite crystals, all of which were also heavily ground on one or more of their flat surfaces. Some appear to have been pressure scratched against something very abrasive, such as sandstone. Two of the pieces show traces of chrysocolla powder. In the bottom right are six round cobbles, all essentially the same color.

In the bottom left are stone projectile points and fragments. The four made of black obsidian are much worn and appear to have been buffed somehow.

The round stone in the center, which is about 2 inches wide and 3/8 of an inch thick, has been smoothed on both faces.

REDS AND YELLOWS

Plate 68

There are hundreds of species and colors of lichens, so only the experienced eye of an expert can call them by name. Several different colors may attach themselves to the same rock, usually on the north side, although many break that rule. Because these strong-colored rocks are a favorite of mine, once a friend told me that if I took one home, kept it inside in a sunny place, and sprayed it with beer once a week, it would continue to grow and keep its fresh colors. It didn't work.

LIFESTYLES

Figure 39

Barton Wright

A room at San Lazaro might have looked like this in prehistoric times. A homemaker on the left is grinding corn on a metate that probably has a coarse surface. She might have moved the crushed kernels to one of the finer-surfaced metates if she wanted to reduce them to cornmeal or even cornpowder.

The woman sitting on the right is making piki bread on a griddle as smoke rises and swirls around in the room looking for a hole in the roof through which to exit. Interior smoke must have been something everyone took for granted.

A traveling bag, two canteens, and several hides or woven shawls hang from the walls.

Plate 69

Because applying fresh adobe was the last step in the construction of a roof, the impressions that were made in the mud can tell us a lot about what materials were used. The grooves in the two clods at the left were made by reeds (latillas) 1/4-inch wide, while in the center are impressions made by cedar bark. Sometimes the builders used split cedar or piñon boards, as is visible in the example at the right.

The layer of adobe mud on the roof was normally about 4 inches thick, and after it baked in the sun for a few days, it became so hard it was almost waterproof. Most of the moisture that is available in the high desert comes from thunderstorms, which can drop water fast, but usually are of such short duration that water would not soak through the roof and into the room below.

Carole Gardner

ROOMS AND VENTS

Plate 71

Vent plugs usually made of adobe were used to close air holes between rooms. In addition to promoting air circulation, the holes served as a conduit through which people inside could communicate.

Plate 70

Rooms 3, 2, and 4 in Building I compose an area that was probably the home of one family, since it is unusual to have three rooms connected by internal doorways. At least one of the rooms would have had an entrance through the roof that allowed light to come in and enhance the white plaster paint on the walls.

Vent holes are common, but this is the only one we have seen so near the floor. Although the stone in the foreground was found in the hole, normally vent plugs such as the one shown in the insert, are made of adobe and come complete with one or more finger holes.

ARCHITECTURE

Plate 72

The architecture of this room, which is more than 6 feet deep, is typical of rooms in Building II. All of the rooms in the pueblo were built with walls above the ground, but only a few of them can be seen today. Over time, as the roofs collapsed, the rooms slowly filled with debris such as dead weeds and blowing sand.

Although the tops of the walls of this room are about 16 inches below the present ground surface, in some buildings the wall tops are covered with only an inch or so of dirt. During a wet spring when the weeds are growing, some walls can be detected by the lack of flora growing on them. Under such circumstances, it is an eerie feeling to plainly see the outline of a room that was not visible the week before.

COMMUNAL ROOM

Plate 73

This room on the north end of Building II, which is 18 feet by 9 feet, is much larger than most living spaces at San Lazaro. It was probably used as a communal work area because four metates with nine associated manos were discovered near the north wall at the right. The adobe storage bin in the corner probably originally contained corn. It likely had a wooden cover that made its contents relatively vermin resistant. Insects and other creatures of the night must have been a constant problem.

The round hole near the bottom of the bin contained a tight-fitting adobe plug with two finger holes to facilitate its removal.

The photo was made seven months after the room was excavated, and although the adobe walls showed no erosion, the floor already had started to go back to nature.

Probably less than 10 percent of the rooms at San Lazaro have doorways that join rooms, and almost none have openings through an outside wall. Normally entrance was gained through the roof, and the occupants controlled the ladder, which gave them an element of security. We guess that each family may have had up to four rooms in a home, and it was sometimes convenient to move about without going outside. Doorways built between rooms were small; for example, one measured only 14 inches high. The idea was to prevent an intruder from coming in with a weapon at ready. If one is entering head first through a small door, he is vulnerable to punishment from those inside.

Seen in this photo are the remains of three rooms and a portal, with its entrance between two vertical rocks. Originally four cedar posts held a thatched roof, and three sides of the small room were left open.

When we completed excavating this complex of rooms in Building I, all of the walls were in pristine condition. After only three years, the ravages of weather and livestock had taken their toll, which prompted us to backfill subsequent excavation sites.

Plate 74

LARGO GLAZE-ON-YELLOW

Plate 75

Jan Orcutt excavated this Largo Glaze-on-yellow bowl (11 inches across and 5 inches high) in Building I, where it was resting upside down about 20 inches deep in the room fill. After she had carefully removed the dirt from around it, she turned it over, and we took this picture. We had no idea that it would be full of ashes, most of which can be seen at right. Between about 1400 and 1450, someone must have been cleaning out a fireplace and used this bowl to carry the ashes away to discard. Why they left the ashes in the bowl will always be a mystery to us. Either they must have been in a hurry to leave or else they felt they had no further use for the bowl. Over time, it had been covered up by blowing sand and dirt.

Jan Orcutt, a professional archaeologist and Southwestern pottery expert, screens dirt that was removed from a room in Building I. Jan spent many hours working with us at the pueblo.

Figure 40

BABY BIRD

Plate 76

This slate eagle, with wings spread as if in flight, was recovered from a room in Building I near where the mask assemblage was located. The outline of the stone appears to have been flaked with a bone tool or the tine of an antler. It could have been made as a talisman with the power to avert evil. Ironically, it was stolen before it was measured, but we guessed its wingspan to be about 4 inches.

BLACK AND WHITE POTTERY

Plate 77

The trash middens on both sides of Del Chorro Creek contain many remnants of black and white pottery vessels that were made before about 1330. Since we have done almost no excavations in the early rooms adjacent to those middens, we have no complete early bowls in our collection. The sherds pictured here, which were recovered in the plaza between Buildings I and II, have designs typical of those that were popular before lead oxide glazes became widely used. The largest sherd is about 8 inches wide.

SURPRISES

It was about noon on a cold winter day in 1989 when Charmay and I were completing the final work in a room on the north end of Building I, not far from where the masks and ceremonial assemblage had been recovered.

Most of the room-fill rubble had been removed, so only the final sweepings remained. A flagstone jar lid, broken in five pieces, was lying on the floor in the southeast corner, but we had seen no reason to move it during our excavation.

Because the wind was brisk, we decided to have our soup and sandwich there in the room where no one had eaten in more than 500 years. It was a rewarding moment, and we were pleased to see this place almost as it had been when new so many years before. One could not help but think of those who had lived here and wonder what their dreams and aspirations might have been. Did they have enough food and water? What did they do for recreation? Our thoughts wandered . . .

While sitting on the floor and leaning against the south wall, I placed my cup of hot soup on the round piece of flagstone. It sounded a little empty and different from what I had subconsciously expected. No matter, I thought, so we enjoyed a short break while the aerial antics of the ravens entertained us, and a red-tailed hawk watched suspiciously from his high soar.

As we rose to leave, Charmay said, "Just for the fun of it, why don't you look under the jar lid?" After considering what I thought was the futility of doing that, against a desire to respond to a somewhat stern question, I carefully removed the five broken pieces of flagstone, one at a time. Before the second piece could be moved, we both felt something different was happening. To our astonishment, we discovered a black, plain-ware jar that had been buried up to its rim under the floor. Inside the jar rested a rectangular, painted bowl, and both of them contained corn kernels. For us, this discovery added a whole new dimension to our knowledge, so we felt elated that we had discovered another aspect of prehistoric life at San Lazaro. Several high-water marks that are prominent in the middle of the black jar indicate that water had penetrated the 4 feet, 10 inches of room fill, from the ceiling to the floor of the room, and entered the jar to a level of 4 inches or more.

A study of the statigraphy of the room revealed that a major part of the fill was little more than rocks that had fallen inward from the walls, rotted wood from the ceiling structure, and sand that had blown in along the way. Similarly, many of the rooms that Nelson excavated in 1912 and left open are still no more than 80 percent filled.

Barton Wright

THOUGHTS TO PONDER:

1. Only one of the thirty-two prehistoric rooms we excavated contained an identifiable corn storage area. Where did all the other families keep their food?

2. Why was one bowl containing corn found inside a larger jar that contained corn?

3. Why did the occupants of the room move away without taking their food?

STILL SURPRISES

Plate 78

The corn storage jar is shown here in situ, buried up to its rim with the flagstone lid, 11 inches in diameter, resting beside it. The jar was buried at a precise depth so that the lid would rest on the dirt and not on the rim itself, yet the fit was tight enough to prevent dirt from entering between the lid and the jar.

Plate 79

After removing the stone lid from the jar, we snapped this photograph, which shows the rectangular bowl inside the plain ware jar. The corn inside had not seen daylight for 500 years or more, and nine roly-poly bugs were scurrying around trying to decide what to do next. We wondered how many generations of these creatures had lived in the darkness of these two vessels just eating, sleeping, and propagating.

Plate 80

The plain ware, corrugated jar above was removed from below the surface of the floor where it had been tucked in snuggly for over five centuries. It is 10 inches wide at the mouth, 13 inches at its belly, and 9 1/2 inches high. It was used as a granary with a flagstone cover that was designed to keep bugs and other vermin from reaching its contents.

Resting inside the plain ware jar was this rectangular bowl, which has a dark galena-glaze dragonfly painted on each end, and sixty-nine dots around its rim. It is 7 1/2 inches long and 2 1/2 inches high.

Plate 81

STONE AXE

Plate 82

Three stone axes have been found partially exposed in the trash mound near Building XV. This one, made from basalt, was showing only a 1-inch portion of the poll at left, so we took our hands and moved the dirt from around it and made this photo.

BASKET SHERDS

Figure 41

Sometimes pottery vessels were formed on the inside of worn-out baskets that had been woven from plant materials. This technique of pottery making was much less labor intensive than making pots by the traditional coiled method. Rings of damp clay were pressed against the inside of the basket, scraped to the desired uniformity, then left to dry and harden. The thin lines on the sherds mark the divisions between adjacent coils of clay.

Because the finished bowl could not be removed from inside the basket before firing, the basket was sacrificed, but left its impression on the outside of the vessel.

Fortunately, such pottery sherds can tell us a lot about how the baskets used were made. Ancestral puebloan potters probably were pleased with the unusual surfaces that were produced in this manner.

ALL-WEATHER WORKERS

Plate 83

Forrest and Jan Orcutt don't let a little weather slow their enthusiasm or stop their work as this photo taken from Building I shows. Jan, who knows a lot about San Lazaro, wears that UCLA jacket every chance she gets.

Plate 84

Charmay and Nancy Reynolds are pictured screening the dirt excavated from a room in Building II. The beautiful Sangre de Cristo Mountains, which rise above 11,000 feet, can be seen on the horizon.

ROOM COLLAPSE

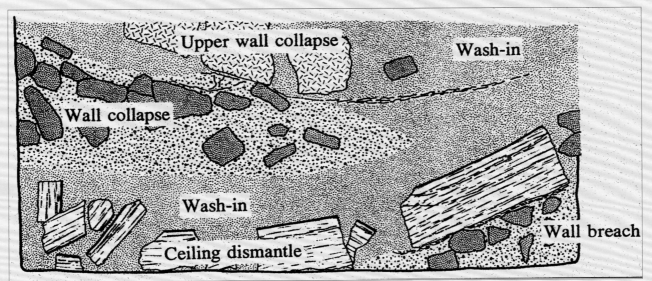

Figure 42 Office of Archaeological Studies

What typically happened to rooms in Building I when they were abandoned and collapsed over time is depicted in this figure. The vigas and other usable building materials probably were pulled out of the rubble for use elsewhere, which escalated the disintegration of the room.

SMALL POTS

The seven little pottery vessels pictured here look as if they were formed by children who were practicing to be adults. The ladle at bottom right is 2 1/4 inches long.

Figure 43

RED AND YELLOW OCHER BOWLS

Plate 85

The little bowl on the left, which is not quite 2 inches square, dates to about 1520, and has red ocher (hematite) clinging to all of its inside surfaces. It was found in Building I. The square bowl on the right, which is 3 3/8 inches wide, has an "X" painted on two sides. It was used in the middle of the fifteenth century to hold yellow ocher (limonite) and still contains some of the powdery substance. It was discovered by Gramly's crew, inverted near a cluster of crystals and other ritual objects near the west wall of Room D in Building XII. It can be seen in situ as object 3 in figure 12, page 31.

STONE BUTTONS

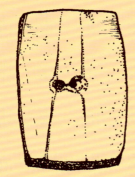 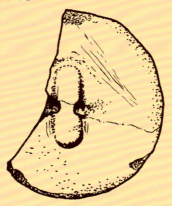

Figure 44

Two prehistoric buttons made of slate are shown here in life-size drawings by Carole Gardner. They both have holes drilled at connecting angles and smooth faces on the reverse sides.

SMALL FETISHES

Plate 86

Fetishes, or animal effigies, are relatively rare at San Lazaro. So far we have recovered only sixteen, three of which were found in medicine bundles; four are made of stone, and twelve are made of fired clay.

In this photograph, the top figure is 2 3/8 inches wide and its feet, where it was once attached to a vessel, have been ground smooth. Charmay found it in Building I. Eric Blinman thinks the flaked, basalt figure in the center is a horned toad effigy, but I think it is a turtle. Jan Orcutt found it in a medicine bundle in Building I. The other figures are made of fired clay.

ENTER THE INVADER

Before 1540, when twenty-nine-year-old Francisco Vázquez Coronado crossed the Rio Grande near El Paso and headed north, the Indians in the Southwest were considered prehistoric, meaning they had no written language. Most were living in large tenement buildings and spoke several different languages. It must have been a wondrous and frightening sight when the natives first saw all of those strange-looking people in stranger-looking clothing sitting astride such tame and gentle-looking animals. I wonder if their reception would have been the same if the natives had known then that the invaders were coming in to take over their country.

Coronado came with a few goats and sheep that were to be used as food, but apparently none of them survived for long. However, in 1598 Juan de Oñate arrived at San Juan Pueblo, north of Santa Fe, with about 4,000 sheep and 1,000 goats. As the domestic animal populations grew, breeding stock began appearing at the nearby pueblos, including San Lazaro. The Indians must have loved these animals because they were friendly, easy to keep and raise, and would eat almost anything that grew and some things that didn't. Additionally, their hair could be woven into a wide array of garments and other items.

Richard Flint and his wife, Shirley, who are the foremost authorities on Coronado, have spent almost a quarter of a century studying his entrada into the New World. Their research has turned up some interesting new facts that debunk many of the time-chiseled beliefs about the expedition. The Flints note that on February 2, 1540, the scribe, Juan de Cuevas, in the town of Compostela, Mexico, made a list of 287 names that included all the persons who were going. Before the expedition could reach the Rio Grande, the number had swollen to 2,000 or more. Some of the add-ons and tag-alongs were European men-at-arms, servants, wives, children, companions, free women, and slaves, who probably numbered eighty or more. The Flints

wrote that at least 800 Indians were recruited from the Valley of Mexico and another 500 or so were added as the force moved through what are now the Mexican states of Michoacán, Jalisco, Nayarit, and Sinaloa.

The exploring entourage had no wagons, and most of the members were outfitted with only native-made weapons and shields. Just forty-five had European metal helmets to wear. The Flints suggest the Coronado expedition looked for all the world like a massive troop of Mexican Indian warriors, rather than medieval knights. Few of its Old World members had been trained as soldiers, although it could be argued that some of the twenty-five men with harquebuses and nineteen crossbowmen may have had previous battle experience.

During the sixteenth century, as the Spanish made at least five expeditions into the Galisteo Basin, they provided us with the first written descriptions of the pueblos and their inhabitants. Historical facts can be quite contradictory when recorded by one person at a time, so the accounts of the day were not precise or complete enough to tell us which of the early explorers actually visited San Lazaro. However there is some evidence that Coronado, or at least some of his men, did visit the site (see page 258).

San Lazaro was off of the beaten track because most of the explorers traveled the major water courses when possible. However, the written history does give us hints about what life was like at various places. The reports of the Rodriguez-Chamuscado party of 1581 mentioned that San Lazaro had about 1,000 inhabitants who were living in eighty multi-story buildings, and that the people cut their hair in the form of a close-fitting soup bowl. The point also was made that the San Lazaro Indians had plenty of corn with which to make flour, called piñole.

The Spaniard Castaño de Sosa, who traveled through the area in 1590, reported that a pueblo that may have been San Lazaro supplied him and his company with provisions of maize (corn), flour, beans, and turkey. It is believed that the San Lazaro farmers provided more than sufficient food for the local inhabitants. Surely that is one reason that the raiding Comanches and other nearby tribes had the unfortunate tendency to visit San Lazaro.

Paul Logsdon took this early morning photo that shows how the ruins of the sleepy historic pueblo and church look dressed in their drab winter coats. In the summer, when there is adequate moisture, this scene would look afire with purple asters, magenta cholla blooms and red Indian paintbrush blossoms. The square in the center comprises Buildings XV and XVI.

Plate 87

STORAGE OLLA

Plate 88

While excavating along the floor of a room on the plaza side of Building XV, about 9 feet below the present ground surface, we uncovered this flat piece of flagstone, 2 feet long. It had rounded corners that we knew had been man-shaped. A well-worn hunch told us there was something under it, but at the time of this photo, we didn't know what. Beside the slab were a large hammer made from petrified wood and a much-experienced floor and wall polisher.

When we removed the flagstone lid, we discovered a large pottery olla that had been placed under the floor.

Plate 89

A hole had been dug below the floor of the room to hold the large olla, which had some pretty serious pressure cracks. A thick layer of grass and ashes had been packed all around the jar for padding, and four large manos had been placed upright, one on each side, to hold it level and steady. A small part of the grass padding can be seen in the bottom of the photo.

Plate 90

The 15-inch-wide olla, after I glued the pieces back together, looked like this. My sloppy job of restoration has since been corrected.

Plate 91

TROUBLE GALORE

The Spanish explorers entered the Southwest with a two-fold mission—to find gold to fill the king's treasury and to convert the natives to the Catholic religion. In so doing, they had been admonished to be gentle with the locals and treat them with respect. In their quest to find gold, the invaders were dismal failures, mainly because few of the Indians had ever seen the metal and none of them knew where it could be found. The desire to convert the Indians, however, met with some success, although many resented being told that they could no longer practice their native rituals.

In 1613, using local native labor and materials, the Spanish erected a mission on the east side of San Lazaro Pueblo and appointed Fray Andres Perquer as its resident priest. Soon conflicts erupted between the church and state over both the use of Indian laborers and the repression of the pagan kachina ceremonies. Governor Pedro de Peralta continually placed levies on the local Indians, requiring them to help construct government offices in the new town of Santa Fe, which had been founded only four years earlier. An angry Fray Perquer wrote to the Franciscan prelate, Father Ordonez, suggesting that he might not allow his Indians to be pressed into the labor force so often. Both priests then wrote to the governor in Santa Fe, suggesting that workers from more distant pueblos, whose inhabitants were rarely called on, should be summoned for the work details to give those from San Lazaro a much-needed rest. Those pleas were largely ignored, and the seeds of discontent were planted.

Then on Sunday, July 7, 1613, the governor arrived at the church in Santa Fe for Mass and found that his chair had been thrown out into the street, an incident that probably evoked a few snickers and a vengeful hint of satisfaction in some quarters. Subsequently the governor, who by then must have been a little overheated, had his chair placed just inside the back door of the church near the baptismal font where the Indians were. While all the other Spanish officials and dignitaries were seated in the front near the high altar, the governor seemed conveniently resolute in his decision to rest by the rear exit.

The next year, when Fray Augustin de Burgos became the guardian at San Lazaro, a convento for his use was erected near the church. However, the mission was not permanent, so in 1621 it became a visita (parish without a resident priest) of Galisteo, and then, in 1638, of San Marcos, when that mission was built.

Between 1618 and 1621, Governor Juan de Eulate encouraged the Indians to resume practicing their pagan traditions, including those of idolatry and concubinage. One of the Indians at San Lazaro, a man named Cristobal, was reprimanded by Father Pedro Zambrano Ortiz for living in sin with a woman. Cristobal replied that the local encomendero (a person authorized to collect tribute), one Juan de Gomez, had promised that he would bring an order from Mexico City that would allow the Indians to return to living as they did before they became Christians, which, to the clergy, meant living in sin.

On September 5, 1660, Governor Lopez de Mendizabal asked that San Lazaro Pueblo furnish ten Indian laborers to work on the Palace of the Governors in Santa Fe. They were to come with prepared wooden boards, gypsum for making whitewash and Indian women to paint the walls. They also were warned to watch for Apaches along the way.

Then, as part of his political struggle with the Franciscans, Mendizabal also decreed that the Indians could resume their ceremonial dances. Of course, that made the Indians happy, and, on occasion, even some of the Spaniards dressed as kachinas and joined in the dancing.

Carole Gardner

On September 27, 1661, in Santa Fe, Fray Nicolas de Villar, guardian of the Galisteo mission, gave testimony before Fray Alonso de Posada about the whole sordid affair. He thought the dances were evil and idolatrous and was appalled that the dances might be spilling over into the Spanish community. He reported that Juana Bernal, an unmarried woman who was a citizen of this town, told him that Ysabel Griego, and her daughter, Maria Gonzalez, Catarina Bernal, and Augustin Griego had been seen doing the kachina dance and had even danced the dance in the pueblo of San Lazaro. Then, afterwards, they had done the same dance in their house near Galisteo with Augustin Griego dancing in the nude.

By the spring of 1680, most of the pueblos were fed up with the overbearing European authority, which they saw as being cruel, unreasonably demanding, and offering little in return but the repression of native religious practices. A very secret and highly organized plan to rebel against the Spanish on August 13 had been plotted for many months. It called for a killing attack against everyone of white blood including men, women and children, and especially against priests and government officials. No one was to be spared.

On August 9, two Indians from Tesuque Pueblo, Catua and Omtua, turned traitors and warned Governor Otermin in Santa Fe that the 2,400 Spaniards in the region were about to be murdered. Otermin, in turn, set about contacting everyone he could find to warn all to flee while there was still time.

Because the cat was then out of the bag, all of the pueblos were quickly given an immediate attack order. The next day, Indians from San Lazaro, who at first had resisted the idea, joined those from other pueblos, 3,000 in all, and marched on the Palace of the Governors in Santa Fe where, on August 11, an all-out battle raged and 400 Spanish were massacred. In other organized efforts, friars were killed at Galisteo, Pecos, and San Marcos Pueblos. Evidently the only thing that saved Santa Fe from total destruction was the tattle-tale warning that had been given to the governor.

Then, on August 20, in one desperate gesture, 100 Spaniards suddenly charged out of the Palace, where they had been cornered, and attacked the Indians, killing about 200 and capturing forty-seven, all of whom were quickly hanged in the plaza. The next day, all of the Spanish who were still alive, including Otermin, began a panicked retreat down the Rio Grande toward Mexico, where they hoped they would find safety.

DISAPPEARING THE SPANISH

So then, after 140 years of domination by the Spanish, the natives rejoiced in their victory and set about destroying all evidence of the intrusive culture that remained, especially those things relating to the Catholic religion. The churches were burned or otherwise destroyed, and brass candelabras and other religious utensils were beaten with clubs and broken into small bits, the parts of which were flung in all directions.

The Spanish language was no longer allowed, and those Indians who had converted to Catholicism were scrubbed in yucca suds to wash away the oppressive stains of Christianity. Heavy rocks were used to break the bronze church bell, the shattered fragments of which were scattered around like trash by the vengeful natives. To date, we have recovered twenty-six fragments of the bell, but we are still looking.

The Indian victory had come with the sweet aroma of freedom that would last for only fifteen years, until the European horde again marched north into the cholla and piñon desert, this time to stay.

Carole Gardner

After the revolt, which had involved most of the Indians in the Galisteo Basin, pueblo political alliances were broken, and San Lazaro was no longer a safe place to live. The few inhabitants who remained probably were driven out by marauding bands of Apaches and Comanches. Many of the natives resettled in a pueblo of the same name (San Lazaro) on the Santa Cruz River near San Juan Pueblo. Later, with the promise of land on which to build a permanent village, some moved to First Mesa at Hopi and built the village of Hano. In exchange for the land, the Tewas promised to defend the Hopis from potential invaders from the east.

BURNED CORN

Plate 92

Ears of corn with the husks still in place were found in a room on the south end of Building XV where they had rested for over 500 years. Although hundreds of ears were recovered, only a few included the husks.

CUT BONES

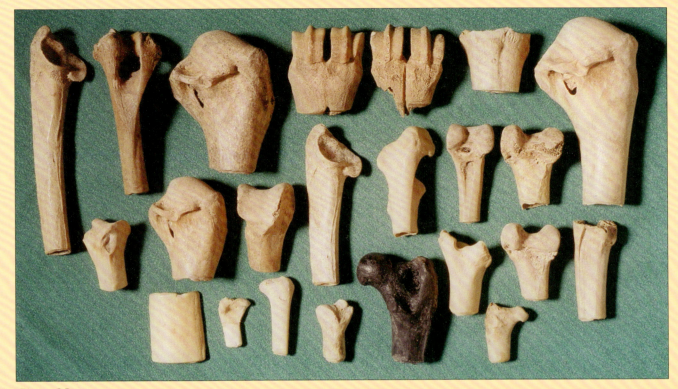

Plate 93

It is always fun to find objects that have been man-made or man-used, especially if they seem to tell a story that makes the mind work a little. These cut bone remnants from the prehistoric side of San Lazaro were probably discarded after being cut for some very specific purpose. We might guess that beads and awls were made from some of them, while others might have been the source of handles for stone knives or other kinds of tools.

FAT BELLIES

It is probable that some of the Spanish population actually had been living in the buildings at San Lazaro with the Indians. When the church was built in 1613, the priest, his servant and other helpers had no other place to live except in the pueblo. By the next year, when a convento was built to house the priest, there was probably an encomendero assigned to manage the pueblo. We think he and his assistants also lived with the natives. Between that time and the revolt, sixty-six years later, a lot of Spaniards must have been cohabitating with the natives. The evidence for that argument is compelling. About 1,420 metal objects of Spanish origin have been recovered from the immediate area of the historic buildings, and that is surely a very small number compared to what is still buried in the 400 or so rooms that have not been excavated. Nails of all sizes and descriptions, which comprise at least half of the metal objects found, could very easily have been used to construct wooden doors for pueblo rooms and to make beds, chairs, and other pieces of furniture.

A close personal relationship between the Spanish and the Indians might explain why there are such a large number of domestic animal bones scattered both in the trash mound and around the perimeters of the historic plaza. The church owned most of the goats and sheep that were probably doled out as rewards to those whom the priests saw fit to favor. But that does not explain why we find such large numbers of cow and horse bones at the site. Perhaps somehow the Indians obtained their own breeding stock. In any event, the inhabitants of San Lazaro had plenty of meat in their soup bowls.

Interestingly, in our work we have recovered two different bison hind-quarters with the big bones still articulated. We think that sometime after about 1613,

San Lazaro hunting parties, perhaps in concert with the Spanish, went out into the Great Plains east of the Pecos River, killed buffalo and brought the meat home on horseback. Without horses, we doubt that such heavy loads would have been transported home.

Plate 94

It is generally agreed that the corn found in the early Southwest originated from native grasses in Mexico and Guatemala. At San Lazaro, it was the main food source as evidenced by the thousands of corn cobs recovered in our excavations. This photo shows some of the different types of food that we have found. The two bones at the left are parts of bird legs, the one on the right, from a turkey. The skull, next to two gourd fragments, is also that of a turkey. In the bottom row are charred corn cobs, beans, a squash stem, piñon nuts, corn kernels and corn kernels still on the cob. In the top row are five peach seeds that were found in the kiva (see page 191). Peaches were probably grown at the pueblo in historic times.

Ash samples taken from a fire pit in Building I contained remnants of both cultivated and uncultivated foods, most notably corn, beans and gooseweed. Other dietary supplements, as revealed by floatation samples, were sunflower, purslane, globe-mallow, clammyweed, tansy mustard and pigweed. Obviously some of these foods are what we call weeds today.

Carole Gardner

FEATHERS AND HIDES

In 1540, when the Spanish explorers came into what is now New Mexico, they found the Indians wearing garments made from woven cotton and the skins of many different animals including deer, elk, antelope, buffalo, mountain lion, and bear. Their blankets were made from either twisted strips of rabbit skins or feathers.

While excavating on the floor of the plaza near the south side of Building XVI, our trowels uncovered a small 10-inch by 30-inch hole that was about 1 foot deep. It had straight sides, a flat floor, and appeared to have been gracefully carved into the otherwise undisturbed plaza floor. Brown rotted wood on its top led us to believe it once had a lid.

Plate 95

The thick clumps of feathers seen on each side of this photo are parts of a blanket that was discovered buried under the floor of the historic plaza, along with fragments of a tanned buffalo skin blanket and two carved wooden "wands." The center object is a 4-inch-long adobe impression of a feather blanket that was found elsewhere in the pueblo. It has a wrapped feather blanket fragment in one of the impressions.

A piece of tanned buffalo skin, about 12 square feet in size (see plate 97, next page) evidently had been carefully folded and placed in one end of the "box". At the other end were the remnants of a compact garment made from both large and small feathers, each of which had been wrapped with vegetal fibers and attached together to form a blanket (see plate 95, previous page).

Both objects were wet and had deteriorated to the point that we had to remove them in small clumps. Hidden in the thick array of feathers were two wooden objects, one of which had been carved on each end (see plate below). Remnants of two corn cobs were also present.

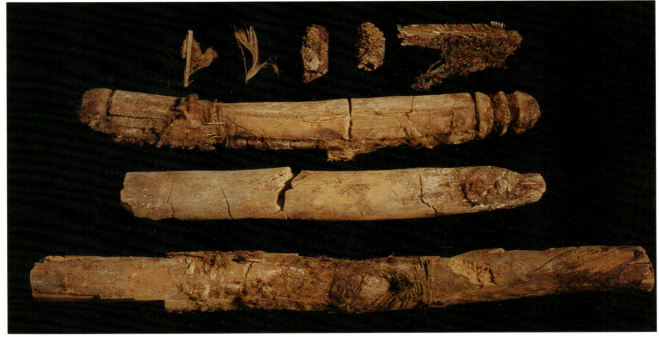

Plate 96

The wooden objects shown in this photo had been wrapped in a feather blanket and buried under the floor of the historic plaza. The top object, which is 10 inches long, has a small piece missing from one end. The carving probably was made by a metal blade, and feathers were tied to it in several places with a vegetal fiber wrap. Originally the middle and bottom fragments were one 28-inch object. Some feathers that still adhere to it probably were tied on. Additional feathers and two corn cobs, seen in the top of the photograph, were found with the objects.

Plate 97

These clumps of tanned buffalo hide are parts of a robe that was found with remnants of a feather blanket and two carved wooden "wands" (see plate 96, previous page). The piece on the right, which is 4 inches long, is one of hundreds of fragments of what had originally been a robe.

MORE MEDICINE

Plate 98

A medicine bundle was found on a ledge in a room on the plaza side of Building XV. Although the bundle comprises sixty-two objects, strangely none were found in the terraced bowl at left, which measures 7 1/4 inches by 5 inches by 3 1/4 inches. Other objects found in the kit include three flutes made from the ulnae of large birds, nineteen shell earrings or pendants, sixteen blue fluorite and quartz crystals, five projectile points, seven fossil shells, two olivella shell beads, seven mother-of-pearl fragments, one piece of chrysocolla, one carved bone tool, one piece of petrified wood, a piece of limestone, one mule deer antler and the terraced bowl. Curiously, fourteen of the objects have deep grooves cut across them.

These bone and antler objects were found in the medicine bundle shown above. The bone at left, measuring more than 11 inches long and 3 1/2 inches wide, was carved from the scapula of a very large animal, probably a buffalo. The handles show extensive polish from hand use, and both sides of the blade have been sharpened to a fine edge. The tool looks similar in style to that of a mescal knife, which was used in the prehistoric Southwest to peel certain types of cactus. One tine of the mule deer antler on the right had been removed by hacking with a metal knife.

Plate 99

IRON TOOLS

Although iron objects were found all around the historic pueblo, most of what we recovered came from the large trash mound around Buildings XV and XVI. Metal detectors were used with great effectiveness down to about 7 inches below the ground surface. Of the 1,029 pieces of iron in the collection, many are so corroded that their original use is unidentifiable.

We soon learned that iron, unlike copper, lead, bronze and silver, when left underground for a few hundred years, becomes so rusted and brittle it can be easily broken.

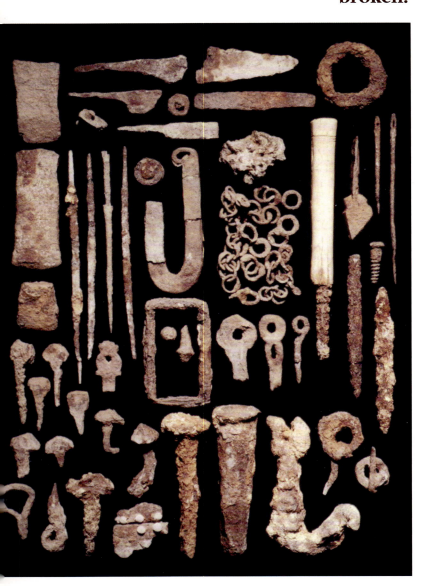

In the top left of the photograph are two chisels, across the top center are three knife blades, in the center are four awls, a strike-a-light (found in three pieces) and multiple pieces of chain mail. In the center right are an awl with a bone haft and needles. In the bottom of the picture are big-headed horseshoe nails, miscellaneous buckle parts, a large chisel and what appears to be a hook.

Probably because of weight constraints, the Spanish did not bring many horseshoes into the new world. For that reason, they sometimes used large-headed nails to affix shoes to the hooves of their mounts. As the horse walked, it wore the heads off the nails, but did little damage to the shoes. When the nail heads became worn, the nails were replaced using the same shoe. It must have been uncomfortable for the animals, especially when they walked on rocks. No horseshoes have been recovered in our work at the pueblo.

Plate 100

Figure 45

The only hafted artifact we have recovered at San Lazaro is this iron awl with a decorated bone handle. The metal is rusted and crumbling, while the bone appears like new. Life-size drawing by Carole Gardner.

Hundreds of nails, awls, and needles have been recovered in and around the historic buildings. In most instances, it is impossible to determine which is which, but we suspect that a majority of these objects are nails.

Plate 101

This Spanish iron chisel was excavated on the north side of Building XVI. Slightly longer than 3 inches, it is one of the few iron objects found at the site, other than nails, the original function of which can be determined.

Plate 102

READING THE RECORD

When Coronado came into New Mexico with his 2,000-man army, he traveled without wagons because no trails or roads had been established. For that reason, his charges were restricted in what they could bring in the way of personal belongings. The rule might have been, "If you can't tie it on your mule, you must carry it on your back or leave it at home."

Then, almost sixty years later, when Juan de Oñate brought Spanish settlers into New Mexico, he afforded himself the luxury of wagon travel. The same was true of four or five other colonizing Spanish expeditions that arrived over the next several decades. By then, each member of the party could bring a wooden chest or leather suitcase that might contain such personal items as toiletries, additional clothing, diaries, and other luxuries. Many such items also were transported in wicker baskets.

It is intriguing now, 324 years after the revolt, to speculate about what a Spaniard, whose name might have been Pedro, who had been living with the natives at San Lazaro, might have thought when he heard the terrifying words that he must flee immediately or suffer the consequences of deadly native treachery. It was the kind of news that would make any Pedro look seriously at his options. Perhaps, in the dark of night, he placed his diary and ledgers in his trunk and secreted it in a nearby, unused and collapsing room, then covered it with rocks and dirt, thinking he would return later and reclaim his trove. For sure, he could not carry those things as he rushed the 300 miles down river to safety.

Historical records suggest that San Lazaro was abandoned at or soon after the revolt in 1680, which lasted just ten days, and that it is probable that Pedro was not so foolish as to return soon for his cached belongings. Actually, he probably was killed trying to escape.

So we think that some twenty-first century archaeologist working in Building XVI will someday uncover a wooden box that contains a diary and some ledger books. Then, for the first time, we may know the names of those who lived in the pueblo, how many animals each owned, and a whole spectrum of details about the daily life at San Lazaro. In our fantasies, we can speculate about how this whole new wealth of information will change the written history of New Mexico. So, is all of this conjecture foolishness??? My hero, Indiana Jones, said, "Archaeology is about facts; if you want the truth, go next door to the philosophy department."

Carole Gardner

COPPER AND BRASS

Plate 103

During and immediately after the revolt of 1680, many of the metal objects that were brought to San Lazaro by the Spanish were broken or severely damaged by the angry natives. This plate illustrates some of the 121 copper and brass pieces that have been recovered from around the historic buildings.

The large piece (top center) is a chisel fabricated from another object. To the right of the chisel are fragments of three gold-plated containers (see plate 106, page 159). Immediately below the containers are six hawk bells. Other objects are a knife blade, an awl and a few nails. The three thin pieces below the chisel are a brass awl with an iron handle, a needle and an aglet or lace tip. The object second down on the left appears to be a spur rowel with two broken points. Similar star-like objects have been found in other early Spanish habitation sites and shipwrecks. In her book, Artifacts of the Spanish Colonies of Florida and the Caribbean, 1500–1800, Volume 2, Kathleen Deagan has illustrations of similar-looking objects and suggests they may have functioned as self-flagellation implements, clothing or saddle ornaments or religious symbols.

Interestingly, thirteen pieces of copper or bronze, 1/8-inch thick, were discovered immediately beneath a 2-foot-high stone. It appears that some determined individual sat on the rock away from the pueblo and tirelessly broke an object apart. The pieces are so mangled that they could not be reconstructed.

BULLETS AND STUFF

Thirty-five bullets, ranging in size from about 25 caliber to larger than 50 caliber, make up about 15 percent of the lead pieces we have recovered. Most of the bullets are unfired, but some show impact damage. As with examples found at other early pueblos, many of the bullets have deep marks made by human teeth, an astounding fact that will likely never be fully explained. Bullets cast from iron and bronze also have been recovered at the pueblo.

Along the top of this photograph are bullets, both fired and unfired. In the middle are two small-caliber bullets still attached to the pouring sprues. In the bottom left corner are a double-sided bronze bullet mold and a copper cross-bow bolt (dart point). The mold (broken on one end) was capable of forming twenty-six bullets in one pouring. Three sizes could have been made, two with tapering points. It is a good guess that the mold was deliberately broken by the Indians during the revolt in 1680.

The heavily rusted iron tool (bottom center), with handles similar to modern-day pliers, was found 4 inches under the ground with a metal detector. It seems likely that it also could be a bullet mold, although its terrible state of disrepair precludes any positive description.

In the bottom right corner of the photograph are two stone flints of the type used to produce a firing spark in the Spanish rifles.

Carole Gardner

Plae 104

LEAD

Plate 105

A superficial scanning with metal detectors on and around the historic pueblo located 232 pieces of lead, many of which are roughly rounded and flat in shape and vary in size from 1 to 2 inches. Their haphazard and nondescript designs suggest that most were meant to be melted into bullets. A number of pieces contain round or square punched holes that might have been used to string them on cordage for transportation or storage. It is probable that at least a few of the round samples could have been made by pounding bullets flat. Others appear to have been made by the spillage of molten metal.

Although no tools such as pouring and lifting shanks, crucibles, clippers, waste ludo, or furnace parts have been discovered at the site, ample sprue and slag specimens provide sufficient evidence that foundry castings of lead did occur there.

Several thin, flat pieces of lead that contain geometric and swirl designs were also found (center right in the photograph). They probably were made by pressing or pouring the metal into a mold and do not appear to have any special use other than to please someone's decorative fancy.

The lead specimens illustrated were recovered mostly in the trash mound south and west of the historic buildings. In the bottom right is an example of slag that had been skimmed from the top of a crucible. Along the bottom left are four sprues that had been cut from a casting.

GOLD AND SILVER

Plate 106

Although the early Spanish explorers came into New Mexico looking for gold, we think they brought more of the precious metal with them than they found when they got here. These three fragments of gold-plated, silver "boxes" were found together after having been deliberately torn apart and mangled, probably by Indians who had rebelled against the Spanish in 1680. The amount of damage suffered by these pieces could not have occurred through normal usage. Our best guess is that all three were parts of reliquaries that held precious religious treasures, such as hair or bone fragments from the body of a saint. The largest piece is 2 inches wide and has very fine, chisel-stamped lines on the back.

SPECIAL TREASURES

Plate 107

Judging by what we have recovered, there must be hundreds of Spanish artifacts still buried in and around the historic buildings at San Lazaro. Pictured here is a small group of a few things that we think are interesting.

The ivory needle was probably imported from China sometime after the Spanish colonized the Philippines in 1565 and started shipping goods through Manila. It is 2 5/8 inches long and was found on the floor of a room. The second object, a silver clasp, is followed by a few of our eleven religious medallions and a broken brass cross.

The Spanish Colonial silver coin, a 1/2-real, which is second from the right in the middle row, was found with a metal detector about 200 feet north of the pueblo. Although the assayer's initials and date are illegible, it was determined by the American Numismatic Society to have been struck between

160

1702 and 1731 in Mexico City during the reign of Philip V of Spain. The hole near one edge would encourage the belief that it was lost while being worn by a casual passerby, since historians generally agree that no one lived at the pueblo much after 1680.

At the bottom left is a heavily corroded copper cross with six green inlays that have facets around the bezels and rounded tops. Lucca, my ten-year-old granddaughter, says the stones are either emeralds or glass, so, of course, we tell everyone they are emeralds.

The object next in line is made of lead, as is the lop-sided cross with the hole in the top. The figure of a man was cast in bronze and, although we have no idea what it is, we think it really is a good one.

Spanish historian Kathleen Deagan thinks the pointed object in the corner is either a locket or a reliquary for safeguarding religious treasures. It was cast in silver and then gold-plated.

CANDLE HOLDER

We think this 1 1/2-inch-wide copper object is part of a candle holder brought to San Lazaro by the Spanish sometime between 1540 and 1680. It was found by a metal detector on top of Building XVI.

Figure 46

EFFIGIES

Plate 108

The purpose of the "human" effigies pictured here has long been a point of conjecture; everyone seems to have a different idea about their use. An acquaintance at Taos Pueblo, who always spoke with his mouth almost closed, informed me that they were only whimsical toys made for children, as he laughed at me for asking the question. He laughed so loudly that I could see he had no teeth in the front of his mouth, which struck me as being funny, so we each had a hearty laugh at the expense of the other.

These objects were made by abrading pottery fragments into the desired shapes. After studying quite a few pieces, we concluded that the paint design made a difference in determining which sherd was selected. Many of the figures look as if they are wearing wrap-around shawls or loincloths.

Similar figures, such as the one in the bottom left corner of the photo, are made of sandstone.

WORKED SHELL

Most of the shell that found its way to San Lazaro came from either the Gulf of California or the Gulf of Mexico and was probably brought in by traders who were looking for turquoise. Our excavations have turned up more pieces of mother-of-pearl (332 pieces) than any other shell, although we also have found olivella, conus, glycimeris, abalone, strombus, spiny oyster, and turritella.

It is obvious that the trading in shell increased significantly after the Spanish arrived, for although we have completed almost six times as much work on the prehistoric side, 82 percent of the shell we have found has come from the historic buildings and the associated trash mound. While there is no direct evidence that Coronado brought shell into the Southwest, since the bulk of the expedition was made up of Mexican Indians, it is likely that they brought worked shell in the form of jewelry and, perhaps, even raw shell to trade or to use as gifts.

Plate 109

The photo shows some of the pendants, beads, and other ornaments found by excavating and surface hunting in and around Buildings XV and XVI. The 4-inch mollusk at the top has been cut to remove a large fragment. The earrings in the upper right were made from spiny oyster.

Barton Wright

BONES AND TEETH

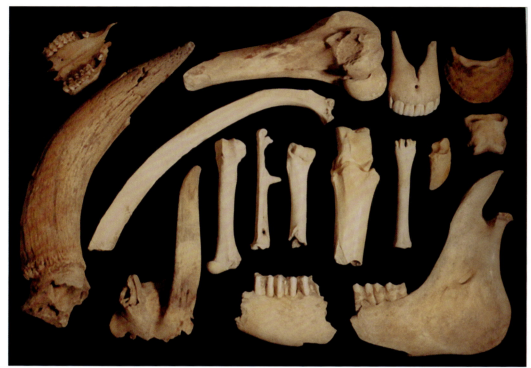
Plate 110

Thousands of bones from both wild and domestic animals litter the room fills in the historic complex at San Lazaro. They can be found in thick layers just inside the plaza, up close to the roomblocks. It appears almost as though someone was eating upstairs and throwing the bones out of a window. An overwhelming majority of the bones are those of goats and sheep. Although we were not able to identify all the types of animals involved, we do have a good sampling. All but one of the bones in this photograph are from either domestic animals brought in by the Spanish or the offspring of those animals.

An exception is the broken right mandible of an adult female buffalo at the bottom right, which was identified by archaeologist Marcel Kornfeld, a high-octane writer from the University of Wyoming, who said, " . . . they hit it several times to open up the marrow cavity. There are also very nice cut marks on the various parts of the ascending ramus, just under the anterior condyle on the coronoid process and about half way down the ramus—clear across from the front to the back." With this simple explanation, now I understand better the value of a good education.

Marcel also identified butchering marks that were made to disarticulate the mandible from the head, noting that the cuts seem to have been made with a metal knife because they are narrow, and usually stone tools leave wider marks.

A horse hoof is in the top right corner adjacent to a set of horse teeth and above a horse toe. The jaw bone in the bottom center is also from a horse, as is the long, diagonal rib bone. The big bone at the top is from a cow, as is the horn core at left. The remaining bones are from goats or sheep (we could not tell the difference) except for the tom turkey leg bone in the very center of the picture. We have hundreds of bones from various animals that are being saved for future study. Of special interest to us are the many goat and sheep leg bones that were broken in exactly the same manner in order to obtain the marrow, the soft, vascular, fatty tissue that fills the cavities of most bones. It was much sought after and highly prized for its protein content.

Grizzly teeth

SOUP BONE

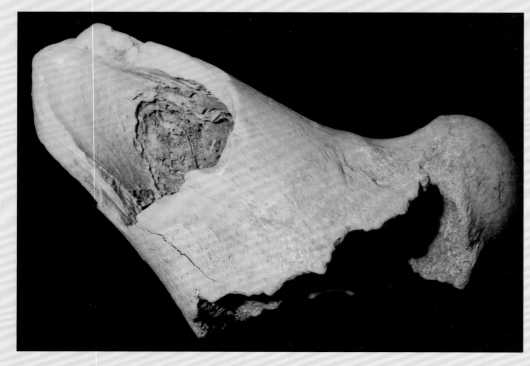

Figure 47

We found this precisely broken piece of a buffalo leg bone in Building XV. Although we have uncovered many bones in our excavations, this one was different from most because all of the edges had been smoothed and highly polished from bouncing around in a pot of steaming soup. Because the inside surfaces of blackware cooking vessels are a little abrasive, it probably didn't take long for this bone to acquire such sheen.

But what can an old soup bone tell us about the people who made the soup? Actually, not much, but a lot of information about ancient diets and nutrition can be gained from the kinds of elements found in the natural residues left behind in cooking pots. Stable isotopes of carbon (13) and nitrogen (15) are particularly useful in determining the amount of meat and plant materials in the diet, because these elements are passed along through the food chain from plants to the animals and humans that eat them.

If we analyzed this bone, we would likely find that it has a high value of stable carbon and a modest value of stable nitrogen, which typically is found in the bones of large, plant-eating animals. More than 400 years ago, the freshly broken bone (and probably several others) was placed in the water-filled cooking pot that was resting in a hearth on the adobe roof of a room. The cook quickly brought the water to a boil by using wooden tongs to remove hot rocks from the fire and gently placing them in the water. It was a constant process of putting hot rocks in and taking the cooler ones out, to be placed back in the fire to reheat. The water prevented the wooden tongs from being burned. As the process was repeated over and over, the hot rocks made the water sizzle, which caused the bone to bounce around. The hot, turbulent water drew the fatty marrow from the bone, slowly making a meat stock or broth.

When the water reached the right viscosity, meat, fresh-picked corn or squash, or both, might have been added, as well as beans, hominy, and grease. The amount of each ingredient depended on what was available, although it probably didn't matter too much. Stew was stew when the kids were hungry. When it was ready, the stew would have been dished into pottery bowls with a gourd dipper, and served with piki, blue cornbread, or corn pudding. They may have also have had hohosi tea, sita (Hopi tea), or a cornmeal drink. Hominy would have been made by sifting wood ashes through a woven tray and into a pot of boiling water to make lye, and adding shelled corn. The mixture was stirred and cooked until the skin slipped from the corn kernels, which caused bubbles to rise. Before adding it to the stew, the corn-turned-hominy was washed in a basket sieve to remove the lye water and bran.

Regardless of the variations in the recipe, the meal would have been quite nutritious providing the diners with protein, carbohydrates, foliates, vitamins A, B6, C, iron, thiamin, niacin, magnesium, high potassium, almost no sodium and only about 500 calories per serving.

Barton Wright

MANDIBLES AND HORNS

Figure 48

A great majority of animal bones uncovered in our excavations, including hundreds of mandibles found inside the historic plaza, are those of goats and sheep.

Figure 49

The Spanish brought many different kinds of domestic animals to San Lazaro, all of which, including horses, were used for food. These goat horns are typical of the hundreds that were discovered adjacent to Buildings XV and XVI in the historic plaza. It was rare to find a goat or sheep skull with horns intact because most of the skulls had been broken open to obtain the brains.

Figure 50

In 1912, Nels Nelson took a photograph that he labeled "Doorway in annex of the church." There is no other record of his work in either the church or the annex at San Lazaro. In the 92 years since the photograph was made, the appearance of the structure has changed enough to prevent us from detecting exactly where this doorway was located.

Neg. No. 27809 Photo. N. C. Nelson, Courtesy Department Library Services, American Museum of Natural History.

Carole Gardner

CHURCH BELL

Plate 111

The church at San Lazaro was built in 1613 utilizing native labor and local stone that was probably recycled from ruined rooms across the creek. Because the church collapsed a few centuries ago, now it is not possible to determine where the bell tower was located, if there was one.

Twenty-six pieces of the bronze church bell have been found scattered around a wide area. We know the rest of the bell fragments are there someplace, so they probably will be found by later archaeologists. Luckily we were able to glue four of the fragments back together.

During the revolt against the Spanish in 1680, Indians broke the church bell and other objects. The hairstyles are accurate as described by a Spanish soldier.

Barton Wright

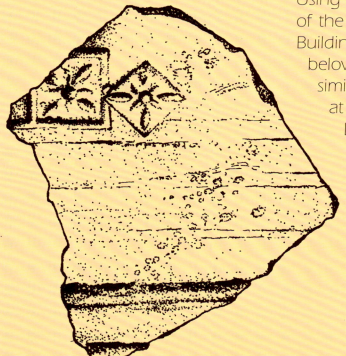

Using a metal detector we located this fragment of the church bell in the trash mound south of Building XVI, where it was resting about 9 inches below the surface. The geometric designs are similar to those on a seventeenth century bell at the Palace of the Governors in Santa Fe. Life-size drawing by Carole Gardner.

Figure 51

These two fragments of the church bell show where rocks thrown by angry natives have left lasting ding marks in the thick bronze. Metallurgists are surprised that the bell could be broken into such small pieces using the tools available to the Indians at that time.

Plate 112

MUSICAL BONES

Several types of musical instruments made from bone have been found at San Lazaro. Objects with multiple holes are either flageolets that are blown from the end or flutes that are blown from the side. They are usually manufactured from the ulnae of large birds such as eagles or red-tailed hawks.

Although one cannot readily determine if an instrument is a flute or a flageolet, the presence of an oval sound window may indicate that the object is a flute. In any event, since we can't tell the difference, we will take the easy road and call all of them flutes. Richard W. Payne, in his article titled "Bone Flutes of the Anasazi," states:

> Ducting material, such as pine pitch, was sometimes placed in the hollow chamber directly below the opening made by the sounding hole so as to direct the air stream toward the back edge of the hole, thus creating a shrilling sound. The placement of tone holes had a direct bearing on the octave range of the instrument. Whether these holes were placed very carefully or haphazardly is not known.

Our excavations have produced thirty-nine flutes, four with three holes, twenty with four holes and four with five holes. Ten others were fragmentary, so the number of holes could not be determined. Holes seem always to have always been placed on the concave side of the bone.

Whistles, which have only one sound hole, usually are made from the radius of a large bird. We have found nine in our excavations.

Pueblo Indians today say that whistles were used to call wild turkeys. Jean A. Jeancon described how they might have been played:

By covering the hole in the side, a different pitch can be obtained. The manner in which they were used is as follows: The opening at the top of the bone is placed tightly against the lower lip, a little below the mouth; then drawing the upper lip down with a slight puckering of the whole mouth, and sucking in with a short, chirping breath, the tone produced will resemble that of a mother turkey calling its young. By careful practice in covering and uncovering, more or less, the hole in the side, and a slight difference in the forming of the lips, it is an easy matter to imitate all the calls of the wild turkey.

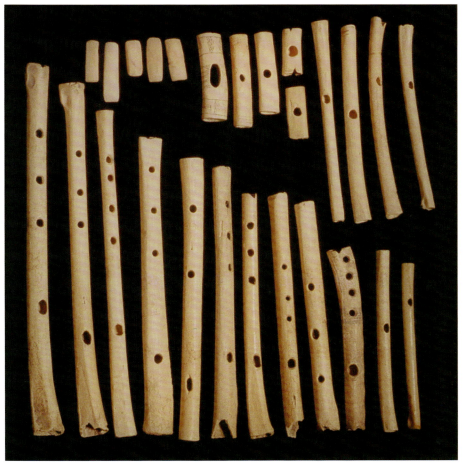

The five short bone objects in the upper left of this photo are bitsitsi whistle halves. Such whistles are made by binding together two concave pieces of bone, with the concave sides inward. An elderly Taos Pueblo hunter told me that sometimes a blade of grass was placed between the bones, bisecting them before they were bound. The whistles could be carried in the mouth, leaving both hands free, and when air was blown into one end, a chilling high-pitched sound, similar to that of a dying rabbit, could be produced. Pueblo Indians today still use a bitsitsi whistle in certain ceremonies.

Plate 113

BONE TOOLS

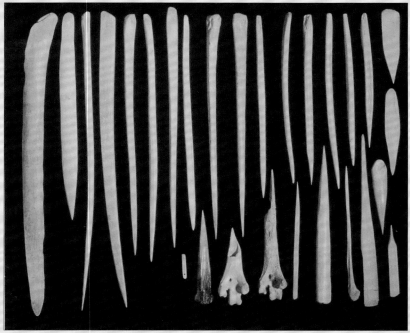

Plate 114

Some of the most frequently found artifacts at San Lazaro are bone tools, especially awls, which were used to make holes for sewing skins, or in weaving baskets or textiles. Of the hundreds in the collection, many have been heavily used for such everyday chores. This photo shows a few examples from the prehistoric roomblocks. After the Spanish arrived with metal, bone became less favored as a raw material for tools. The object on the left is 9 inches long.

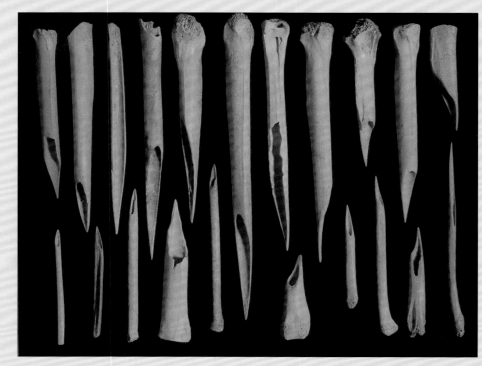

Plate 115

Awls made from the hollow bones of birds are generally sharper than those made from the bones of other animals. So many have been recovered in our excavations that we think the Indians must have been able to kill birds of all sizes with comparative ease.

Plate 116

The hundreds of tubular bone objects recovered at San Lazaro have been found in all sizes, as this photo reveals. The smaller ones may have been beads that were strung and worn around the neck. After a rain, the longer tubes probably were used as straws with which to suck water from the many shallow indentations that are found in the rocks around the pueblo. Water must have been very precious, so we think it was stored in pottery containers for later consumption. The longest bone is just over 6 inches.

Carole Gardner

At San Lazaro there was ample bone available for making tools, especially after the Spanish arrived with domesticated animals. The exact use of many of the tools illustrated will forever remain a mystery, but one might speculate that some of them were used for weaving, scraping and smoothing unfired pottery vessels or for perforating materials such as wood and leather. The tool at left is just under 9 1/2 inches long.

Plate 117

CANINE COUSINS

By 7000 BC, dogs were all over the Americas, and sometimes were even buried with humans. In the prehistoric Southwest, they were used by the Indians for protection, to guard the fields at night, as food, for hunting and for keeping warm, of course.

In her book, <u>A History of Dogs in the Early Americas</u>, Marion Schwartz states: " . . . the Spanish brought huge dogs trained on human flesh with them to the Americas to control native populations. In reading the sixteenth century accounts of these 'hero' dogs, it became clear to me that the Conquistadors regarded their dogs as more noble and intelligent than the people they were conquering."

Our excavations certainly did not uncover any evidence of those particular animals, and it is doubtful that any even came this far north. There is, however, an abundance of information about other early dogs in the Southwest. Two were buried with humans in White Dog Cave in Arizona around 100 AD, and the Mimbres Indians in the southern part of New Mexico painted dog designs in their bowls.

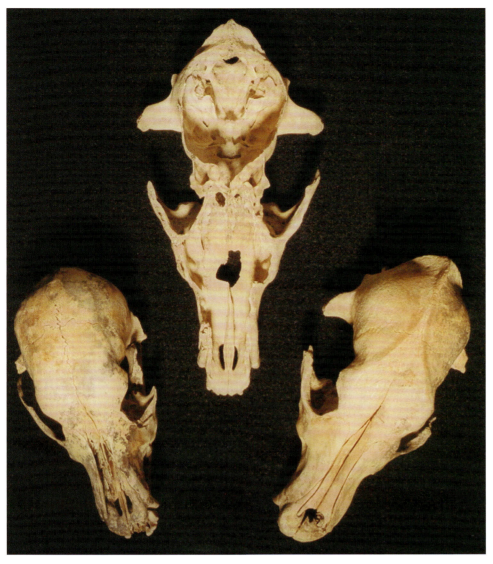

Plate 118

It has not been common to find remains of dogs at San Lazaro. The three skulls pictured here were found in what had been a holding pen for sheep and goats. The pen, which was made of adobe and stone, was 4 feet, 6 inches high, 5 feet wide, more than 17 feet long and abutted the first rooms inside the plaza on the west side. The little corral evidently was used to protect small animals from coyotes, grizzlies, wolves, and other predators that prowled around the pueblo at night.

In the pen were a great number of bones that evidently had been tossed in by humans after most of the meat had been removed. Intermixed with the bones, many of which had been gnawed by medium-sized animals, was a layer of goat and sheep droppings more than 6 inches thick. Of course we had to save samples of the dung.

The skull on the left is from a small, female, European dog; the one on the right is that of a male Anasazi dog, and the one in the center is that of a coyote. While there is no evidence that these animals had been eaten, we are suspicious since no other canine bones were found with the skulls.

Carole Gardner

Evidence of dogs having been eaten by humans in prehistoric times has been found at Grasshopper Pueblo, Arroyo Hondo, and Canon de Chelly, all in Arizona. Since at San Lazaro there seems to have been ample food at the time of occupation provided by both domestic animals and members of the deer family, it may be that these creatures had not been eaten by humans, but the heads had been deliberately placed as offerings.

The only identifiable dog bone found in a prehistoric context at San Lazaro is a rasp made from a femur that was found in a room on the north end of Building I (see figure 20, page 57).

SERIOUS MEDICINE

We were excavating about 12 inches above the plaza floor where it abuts the 9-foot-high east wall of Building XV. It was late in the afternoon, and 45-mph winds lifted the sandy dirt and swirled it around us. The ravens were all grounded, and the sturdy arms of a giant cholla were wildly swaying in the desert wind. For a while I thought I would lose what was left of my hair, and I dreamed that night about not doing that again.

The wall that loomed above us was well constructed with flat latite rocks aligned straightly from bottom to top, except for one, which jutted out of the wall for 6 inches or more. On its flat surface stood a solitary white bear (see figure 52, next page) facing out. As we carefully troweled in the soft dirt below the bear, other wonderful objects began to appear before us (see plates 119, page 181; 120, page 182; and 121, page 183).

We had recovered thirty-seven objects of medicine when I noticed two small pieces of silky cloth (see figures 55 and 56, page 184) blowing back and forth in front of me. I quickly secured them in a Ziploc bag, not knowing for sure what they were. We then surrendered to the growing darkness, not wanting to hurry our work or miss some clue to this important cache of objects. At first light we were back at work, of course.

The white bear fetish pictured here was found standing on a rock about 12 inches above the medicine bundle.

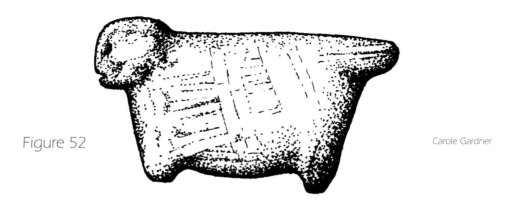

Figure 52   Carole Gardner

The geological background of the bear is interesting. Millions of years ago, as soil and water mixed in New Mexico's karst region, it formed a weak acid, which dissolved the limestone and carried it downward through small fissures in the rock until it reached Carlsbad Cavern. Drip by drip, minute bits of the dissolved stone were left behind on the ceiling and floor in the form of a mineral crystal, called calcite. In time, the calcite crystal grew downward from the ceiling like a stone icicle, called a stalactite, or upward from the floor, a stalagmite. Sometimes a stalactite and a stalagmite grow together to form one column, which is called a speleothem.

This bear fetish was carved from a piece of such calcite, but it is uncertain if the crystal originated as a stalactite or a stalagmite. Its highly polished surface shows the delicate details of how the crystal grew underground, and the white-to-cream color is the result of minute chemical impurities.

Almost all American Indian tribes have a story about a supernatural bear that has a heart of ice which turns to stone in his lodge, a cave. We like to think an ancient Indian from San Lazaro entered the lodge of the bear, ventured deep beyond the reaches of sunlight, broke off a piece of crystal, which looks like ice turned to stone, and used it to carve the bear.

It is one of the rare examples of an artifact that provides a direct connection between elements in the real physical world, a cave and a bear, and the mythological world of American Indian folktales.

To the Navajo, Apache, and some neighboring tribes, the bear's stone heart functioned as a guardian spirit or patron that blessed them with its spiritual power. For the people of San Lazaro, the stone bear was placed to guard the medicine bundle, which probably rested on a portable altar. Life-size drawing by Carole Gardner.

Plate 119

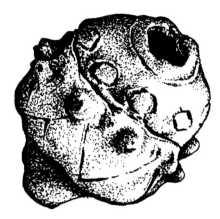

Figure 53

This unusual clay pipe was found with the medicine bundle in Building XV, Room 3. We had not seen anything like it before, and we think it was made for some very specific purpose. Burned tobacco dottle still lingers in the bowl after 400 years of resting in the ground. The design of the pipe reminds us of a peyote plant.

Figure 54

A peyote plant (Lophopora) drawing by Carole Gardner.

This photo shows some of the medicine that was being guarded by the white bear. Across the top are fossil shells that include brachiopods, a pelecypod, two mollusks, and a crinoid. Note the hole that had been drilled in the shell at top right. In the second row are a ceremonial spear point with serrated edges that was flaked from a piece of slate and ground on both faces, a 2 5/8-inch projectile point made from Utah agate, a large projectile point made from Jemez Mountains obsidian, a small brown dart point made from petrified wood, and two corner-notched, Williams archaic dart points dating from 4000 BC to 1000 AD that must have been picked up someplace else.

In the bottom are sixty-eight small fragments of galena, a lead ore that was used to make glaze paint.

Plate 120

More pieces of the medicine bundle are included in this photo. The top two bones are left and right ulnae (wings) of a large bird that have not been altered by man. The second two bones are 7-inch-long flutes with elongated sounding holes that also were made from the left and right ulnae of a large bird. Both instruments still contain pine pitch in their sounding holes, which produce music when air is blown across them.

The third layer contains twelve quartz crystals (silicon dioxide), three rounded chalcedony medicine stones, a round iron concretion, a 5/8-inch bone tube made from the radius of a large bird, and a bone splinter awl.

The bottom two rows contain two mother-of-pearl earrings 2 1/4 inches long, a mother-of-pearl pendant, two quartz crystals, two blue fluorite crystals (calcium fluoride), pieces of rubbed azurite (hydrated copper carbonate) and limonite (hydrated iron oxide), a mother-of-pearl fragment, two pieces of selenite (gypsum), a small red rectangular piece of orthoclase (potassium aluminum silicate), three small pieces of amazonite (microcline feldspar), a small turquoise bead, three incisors of a vegetarian animal (probably a goat or sheep), and a small white triangular projectile point made from a fine-grained quartz. The object at the far right is a 2 5/8-inch iron awl, which indicates the date of the medicine kit is between 1541 and 1680.

Plate 121

Figure 55

After the church was built at San Lazaro in 1613, the Spanish Crown began supplying the resident friars with imported sackcloth (utilitarian woolen cloth) and other fabrics including Chinese and Mexican silks. For example, in 1624 a shipment that arrived with supplies for all of the missions contained 2,600 yards of wool cloth, twenty-six pounds of thread, Mexican blankets, linen shirts, leggings, Turkish carpets, silk cords, and other textile goods. Also included were fabrics of silk decorated with damask and lace.

In her dissertation on the subject, Laurie Webster wrote: "The first places where pueblo peoples had close and sustained contact with imported fabrics were the missions. Most of these fabrics were fine, luxurious items made in far-away places such as Central Mexico, Europe, China, or the Philippines." She went on to say that "things of divine worship," including garments with fringes of silk, were issued to the mission priests.

Kathy Whitaker and Webster, both experts on early Southwestern textiles, have suggested that the two fragments pictured here (magnified 120 percent) are parts of a "finely-woven, commercial plain-weave, silk ribbon, which was made of unspun bundles of fiber that are now highly degraded." The fabric, which may have belonged to the priest at San Lazaro, is probably of Chinese origin and was made sometime after 1565 and before 1680.

It is more than interesting that such a fabric would be part of a medicine bundle that also contained quartz crystals, arrowheads, bone flutes, and fossil mollusks that are millions of years old.

One of the silk fragments pictured in figure 55, is shown here magnified ninety times. The weft and warp counts are ninety-two per inch.

Figure 56

The original photo of the historic side of San Lazaro Pueblo, which was taken in October of 1912 from across Del Chorro Creek near Building II, shows two of archaeologist Nels Nelson's horses peacefully grazing on the sparse foliage west of Building XV. Although piñon trees and junipers are coming back strongly on the distant hill, only sand and rocks are in the immediate vicinity of the pueblo.

Neg. No.15946, Photo. N.C. Nelson, Courtesy Department Library Services, American Museum of Natural History

Figure 57

Plate 122

In 2000, Charmay took this photo to mimic the one Nelson made of the same subject, eighty-eight years earlier (see figure above). There are many more trees near the far ridge, and blown-in sand has covered the old Del Chorro streambed, which has moved 300 feet to the west, so it cannot be seen at the bottom of the picture. Cholla cacti now dot the remains of Buildings XV and XVI.

Figure 58

A 1913 view of the historic pueblo ruin, taken from just outside the southwest entrance, is not very impressive. The rock rubble in the background and on the right is what remains of the U-shaped Building XVI, while the rocks in the middle of the picture and at the left are the remains of the south end of the historic part of Building XV. The dirt in the bottom of the picture, which is mostly devoid of rocks, covers a number of rooms that were occupied between 1440 and 1525.

Neg. No. 128794, Photo. N. C. Nelson, Courtesy Department Library Services, American Museum of Natural History.

Carole Gardner

Plate 123

This photo looks at the south side of what remains of Building XVII, which was three stories high and may have had six or more rooms across the top. At one time, this was a beautiful apartment complex with hundreds of people doing the everyday chores that gave them a decent standard of living. When the site was abandoned shortly after the Pueblo Revolt, its walls started collapsing as ceiling beams rotted and roofs fell in on floors below, also causing them to collapse in a heap of stone and adobe rubble. Time continued its work. Winds blew dust and sand in on top of the mounds. Small rodents living in burrows under the rocks brought home cholla seeds, which germinated, grew, reproduced, and died, resulting in the present-day landscape. The story of a thousand lives will be told when future archaeologists turn the tattered pages of this roomblock.

Figure 59

A 1912 photo, which faces west toward the prehistoric buildings across the Arroyo del Chorro from Building XV, shows the ruins of the stone enclosure that Nelson labeled a lime kiln on the map he made of the site. Although there is a small amount of lime on the ground, we think the structure was a corral for horses and other large domestic animals. The wall must have been at least 5 feet high, judging by the number of rocks that have toppled. There is still the outline of two small rooms on the north side of the enclosure, just inside the entrance, which originally was probably gated.

Neg. No. 27808, Photo. N. C. Nelson, Courtesy Department Library Services, American Museum of Natural History.

SANDSTONE SCULPTURE

Plate 124

Everyone who sees this sandstone "sculpture," which is located about 80 yards west of Building I, has a different idea about how it was made and how it might have been used. Some believe an imaginative Indian artist pecked out the indentations with a stone axe, while others are sure it is just another one of nature's unexplained phenomena. I am still thinking about this one.

DESIRE TO KNOW

In 1988, the San Lazaro Corporation contracted with the Museum of New Mexico and Southern Illinois University to do archaeological work at the site. At that time both a survey was made and about 37,000 artifacts were collected. In addition, significant quantities of macro botanical and zoological specimens were recovered from several test excavations. It was hoped that the investigators involved would use the collected data to reconstruct historic subsistence patterns and dietary changes in the early historic period. To date, that has not happened. It seems that the tree grows slowly, so the earth must be patient.

HILLTOP SHRINE

What we call the "hilltop shrine," is named for its location on a hill a short distance north of Building XVI. During the 3-minute walk up either of two arroyos that lead to the shrine, one can see small pieces of selenite eroding from the banks and sparkling in the sun. This is one of three areas at the pueblo where veins of selenite are exposed.

Plate 125

Immediately west of the shrine is a large, sandstone slip-and-slide, the product of an ancient earthquake. Intense pressure and heat caused by the movement melted the surface of the sandstone turning it into glass. A much smaller slip-and-slide, along with a ten-pound concretion, is still part of the shrine. A Spanish cast bronze religious medal was recovered from the shrine with the use of a metal detector.

The large rock at the right side of the photograph is the petrified trunk of a tree. When a group of eight Tewa-Hopi elders visited the shrine, one of them asked, "Where is the petrified wood?" He went on to explain that all shrines were supposed to contain at least one piece. I remembered seeing the tree trunk a short distance away, so we gathered up three strong men and rolled it into the shrine. I think it was there originally and was somehow moved.

This shrine contains three small enclosures, each having been made of large, well-shaped igneous rocks that had to be moved up the hill and set in place.

KIVA STORY

While working with trowels in the historic plaza where it abuts the south side of Building XVII, we accidentally uncovered the top of a curved wall, something we had not seen before in our excavations at San Lazaro. Further investigations proved that our first impulse was correct; it was the wall of a kiva. Over the next two months, our work slowly progressed to unlock the secrets that had rested dormant in that place for five centuries—or more.

Plate 126

The 8-foot-high north wall of the kiva is impressive. Initially we made a rock and earthen berm around the rim to prevent water from running down the wall. Later, a shelter was erected to protect the murals, the best fragments of which are on the wall behind the juniper post and cannot be seen in this photograph.

The juniper post was anchored in a 2-foot-deep hole, which was about as deep as person could reach to remove dirt.

The large hole in the wall (at top right) was discovered sealed up with rocks and broken mano and metate parts that had been mortared in place and disguised to hide their presence. Behind the opening is a chamber that is 3 feet, 9 inches deep, 2 feet, 1 inch wide, and 2 feet, 10 inches high. It was discovered when a long stick was used to probe into an ominous-looking 1 1/2- inch hole. A careful screening of the chamber dirt revealed a few peach seeds, yucca and squash seeds (two types), and five burned corn cobs. Because only food remnants were recovered from the chamber, we can only wonder why so much effort was made to disguise it.

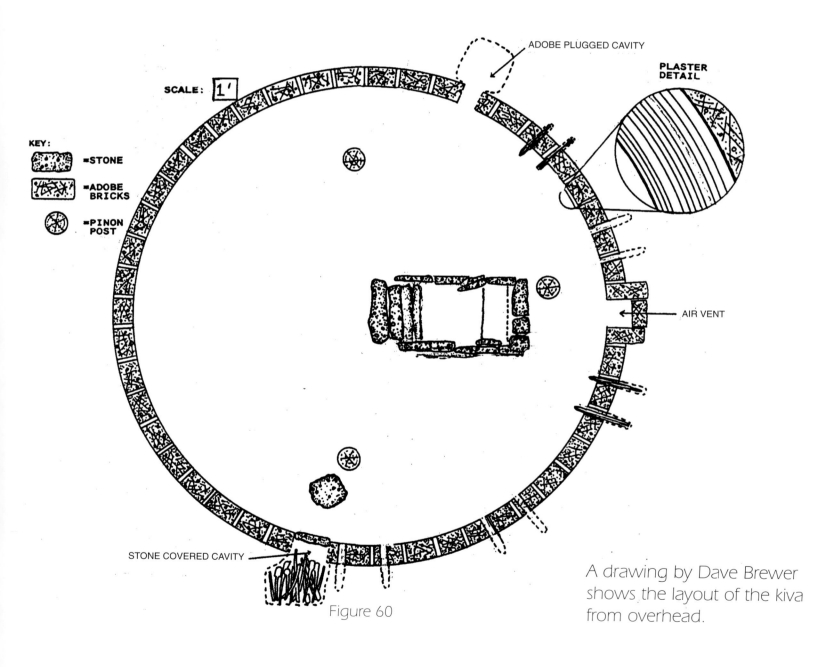

Figure 60

A drawing by Dave Brewer shows the layout of the kiva from overhead.

Richard Blake, Susan and Perry Fishback, Mike Kammerer, Jann Arrington Wolcott, Nancy Bloch, Dee Breckhausen, and Charmay Allred were our main helpers in this venture. As the story of the kiva began to unfold before us, we were struck by some of its unusual features. One was the volume of roofing material, which we think was primarily ponderosa pine vigas, each of which must have been at least 10 inches thick. As the vigas had rotted over time, the roof had collapsed, falling in at various angles and leaving a tan-colored wood-rot more than 3 feet thick in most places.

Soon the tops of three juniper posts, each about 7 inches in diameter, appeared at varying distances, all having been placed about 3 feet from the wall. Originally they had supported the roof. Although one of the posts had disintegrated as it dried when exposed to the air, the other two stood strong and straight. A sample cutting from one of the posts was sent to the Laboratory of Tree-Ring Research at the University of Arizona in Tucson. The lab could tell us when the post had been cut, which might be the same year the kiva had been built. Eric Blinman thought maybe the posts were recycled from abandoned houses across the creek. The lab reported that, "Although it's not possible to accurately estimate the number of sapwood rings removed by decay from the exterior of (the sample), it's unlikely that the tree possessed more than 100 sapwood rings. Therefore, the outermost ring probably would date somewhere between 1475 and 1500."

So, the juniper post had been cut from forty to sixty-five years before the first Spaniard arrived at San Lazaro, meaning the kiva had probably been built in late prehistoric times.

When the kiva began to fall into disrepair, it evidently was used as a place to discard trash, even before the entire roof fell in. As we slowly removed the fill, we recovered thousands of pot sherds, lithics, and animal bones such as those of Spanish sheep, goats, horses, and cows.

Our best working tools for removing the softly packed room fill were small garden hoes with foot-long handles. We recovered two glass beads along with several bone awls, about twenty metates (mostly broken), forty-two manos (also mostly broken), and a beautiful red fibrolite axe that Jann uncovered about 2 feet below the surface on the south side.

The kiva wall was built with adobe blocks, mostly rectangular, about 6 to 12 inches wide and 3 to 8 inches high. Thin layers of adobe mud had been applied to the wall, and marks left by fingers moving across in short swipes are evident in great abundance. Then, somehow the wall was heavily soot-blackened, although we found very little charcoal in the kiva.

As we worked deeper into the kiva, the damp wall around the top began to dry in the wind, and some of it fell away to reveal at least fifteen thin layers of adobe that had been applied to the original wall at various times. Some layers were so thin they were almost indistinguishable.

When we were about 4 feet deep, the thick layer of rotted wood disappeared in some areas, which told us we were below the level of the roof and beam collapse. The south half of the kiva fill was left intact, from top to bottom, until Eric Blinman and Steve Post could record the statigraphy that would show us exactly how the roof had collapsed and where it had fallen in.

The floor was black and hard, but devoid of artifacts save a single mule deer antler that was found near the juniper post on the north side of the kiva. Although we recovered over 26,000 pottery sherds in the room fill, not one was found on the floor that might help us date the kiva.

Juniper limbs 3 inches in diameter protruded from the wall in a number of places. They were placed 6 feet

above the floor, which is an ideal height to hold the top stay of a loom. One of the limbs was stuck into the wall 25 inches.

A large stone and adobe altar stood near the east wall about 3 feet from the air vent, where it dominated the space. The ashes from long-dead fires still occupied its hearth built into the east end of the altar.

Plate 127

A large vent on the east wall of the kiva brought air from the outside, which was disbursed upon reaching the flat, vertical face of the altar 3 feet, 9 inches away. The sides and top of the opening had been shored up with split juniper slats that were still in place. A hearth still containing ashes is inside the rectangular altar at the left end. Smoke from fires rose to exit through the kiva entrance, most likely through the roof.

The outside dimensions of the altar are 5 feet, 2 inches by 3 feet, 1 inch. Split juniper boards 2 feet, 4 inches high and 2 1/2 inches thick frame the inside of the air vent where it enters the kiva.

Plate 128

In this close-up of the south wall of the kiva is an unusual feature that was constructed 2 feet, 1 inch above the floor. When this photo was made, we had no idea what it was or what purpose it served. Maybe it was nothing at all, but it certainly looked strange. A closer inspection revealed the outline of a round adobe plug that can be seen immediately above the horizontal stone (see plate 129, next page). A similar plug below between the vertical stones cannot be seen in this picture.

To the right in the photo near the cedar post is a hole that, at first, did little to attract our attention (see plate 133, page 202). There were so many mysterious things about this kiva that our minds were floating in all directions, and we hardly thought the hole was anything important. Besides, there were numerous holes at varying heights in the curved wall. Note the size of the adobe bricks with which the kiva wall was built.

All of us who toiled to uncover the long-hidden secrets of this sacred place feel a deep and lasting reverence and appreciation for those who must have had profound religious beliefs and practiced their rituals in this underground chamber. It is, indeed, a humbling thought that constantly reminds us to be respectful and considerate of those who lived and worshiped here. Yet, at the same time I have the distinct feeling

Plate 129

A round hole, 5 inches in diameter, appears above the horizontal stone altar. Below the stone is another hole 1/2 inch smaller. Both were sealed with adobe plugs. Two bird bone tubes, each about 1 3/4 inches long, and a small piece of heavily rubbed hematite can be seen in situ in the bottom hole. Other artifacts that were found in the lower hole are a 7 1/4-inch leg bone of a large bird, a hard, round, adobe ball 1 1/2 inches in diameter, three bone awls, two heavily used pecking cobble stones, a piece of selenite 1 1/2 inches long, two unidentified crystals, a white quartzite stone that had been heavily rubbed with red paint, and a small amount of limonite (yellow ocher).

that the spirits of those humans, long departed, are pleased to have us learn a small part about how they lived and who they were. Those same spirits are surely laughing at us now, with the knowledge that most of what they knew then will always remain a mystery to us. So it is with all of us who are fascinated with ancient peoples and seek more and more to quench a thirst for knowing about who they were, thus enhancing our knowledge of ourselves.

When all the debris had been removed from the kiva, and the last of the sweepings were in the dustpan, we climbed the ladder to take a look down at this most magnificent place. The inside of the kiva looked so mystical. The floor and walls were soot-black with a faint, white, 3-inch stripe that ringed the circumference about 4 feet above the floor.

The excavation had taken weeks of hard work. Hundreds of large rocks had to be carried up the ladder or thrown out. The buckets of dirt seemed to get heavier and heavier as we dug deeper. But finally it was done, so we took many photographs. As we rested, we could not have known that our work in the kiva had just begun.

Eighteen teenagers had just arrived from Wyoming, having come to San Lazaro to camp for several weeks and excavate under the direction of George Zeimens, a professional archaeologist, and his wife, Geri. Soon they were all in the kiva, wide-eyed with wonderment. Sharp-eyed teenager Perry Fishback spotted a curious yellow swirl of paint on the north wall that had recently been exposed when a small piece of the layered wall had dried and fallen off. It looked like a shield with some vertical white decoration. Other students began to see faint splashes of red, then black, green, and more white and yellow. It was obvious to us that before the kiva had been abandoned, one final layer of adobe mud had been applied to the wall to hide the murals. Only with the drying of the wall and the peeling of the layers were we finally allowed to see some of the painted designs.

It didn't take long to realize that a whole new story was there before us, begging to be read, so we quickly erected a shelter in the kiva to protect the paintings from the rain and wind.

When first discovered, this "shield" design was only a small splash of yellow paint on the wall. After an hour of careful work, Perry Fishback was able to expose a large portion of the design.

Plate 130

Blake's copious field notes, roughly written at the time, state, in fragments:

> . . . fifteen layers of plaster are discernable by counting in thick edge pieces . . . red & white murals are beneath the completely black layer . . . the orange & white "shield" is a few layers out from the "#9" black layer . . . the red arrowhead on the N wall, pointing W along the tops of the rectangular murals, is on an outer completely black layer . . . there is some green paint on the wall.

His notes went on and on, page after page, as he recorded every little detail that we observed. As the days passed and more layers of the wall dried and fell away, other designs became apparent. We knew that it was just a matter of time until they were gone, so we took numerous photographs as each new design appeared. Our problem was that many thin layers, some of them painted, would fall off the wall in 6- or 8-inch patches, so we could not tell how they related to other layers and similarly colored designs even as close as 2 feet away. We had ample advice from professional archaeologists, but in the end the futility of our efforts became apparent. Many of the mural designs were lost, but we found solace in the knowledge that nothing we could have done would have saved them.

A secret chamber was accidentally discovered on the south wall. When its hidden door was opened, we found it full of wonderful carved wooden objects. As we began to remove them, one at a time, my mind conjured up a long-lost scene of dancers using these "wands" in such a manner that we can only dream of and never know. All of the wooden pieces were carved, some looking faintly like drum sticks. One was carved as an eagle's foot with three sinister-looking claws. Another had a flat, terraced design not unlike what we had seen on so many of the small pots and slate ceremonial objects that had been part of the medicine excavated less than 100 feet to the east of where we stood. Remarkably, half of a bow was recovered from the chamber. It was a most curious find, since bows seldom are found in ancient pueblo contexts. Had it have been deliberately broken or "killed," as were the three kiva bells and a phallus that had been recovered from the stone altar just a few feet away? The mysteries mounted.

Over time, water had penetrated the ceiling causing many of the wooden objects to be muddy on the bottom. Curiously, nine peach seeds were screened from the chamber dirt, and since fruit trees had been introduced into the Southwest by the Spanish, we also know the kiva had been used during historic times.

The white splash on the west wall of the kiva disguised an adobe plug that was similar to others we discovered around the wall.

Plate 131

When the 4½-inch adobe plug was removed from the west wall of the kiva (see above photo), an air tunnel, similar to others on the north and south walls, was revealed. Behind it, a horizontal passageway penetrated about 1 foot, 4 inches, then turned vertically 4 feet, 9 inches to the surface of the plaza.

Plate 132

SECRET PLACE

Plate 133

The kiva was clean, and we were admiring our work when I jokingly asked the five-year-old daughter of a friend to stick her hand in the hole "to see if there are any rattlesnakes in there." To my amazement, when she did her arm went all the way in to her shoulder. I couldn't believe it. The little girl had a big grin on her face, and somehow I wasn't too flattered.

After we slightly enlarged the hole, the beam of a flashlight revealed a deep chamber that seemed to go on forever. Was this just an aberration, maybe an old animal burrow of some sort, or could this be an important feature that we had overlooked? A flagstone slab can be faintly seen to the right and below the hole. It had been caulked into place with adobe mud and then camouflaged with more mud to disguise its existence.

After discussing the situation at some length, we decided that Richard Blake should take trowel in hand and carefully remove the adobe caulking that held the stone in place. Maybe it was a secret door which, when opened, would provide some answers. Little did we know that the mysteries of this sacred place were about to increase dramatically.

Plate 134

As Richard carefully worked to remove the adobe caulking, each step along the way would be recorded with notes and four cameras. The tension mounted as those present, including the teenagers from Wyoming, gathered closely around. Even the wind was still as we watched and waited.

As the work progressed, the flagstone slab or "door" was revealed. It had been shaped to about 15 inches by 16 inches to close the opening into the chamber.

So, it had finally come down to this, and I suddenly knew how Richard Wetherill must have felt the first time he climbed down the rock cliffs, in 1888, and into the ruins of Mesa Verde. No one is immune to that kind of excitement and anticipation.

Plate 135

Richard removed the remaining adobe so the flagstone slab could be carefully lifted away. Secreted inside the darkness was a squarish storage chamber 4 feet, 8 inches deep and just as wide. This is the first photograph of the chamber, taken immediately after the slab had been removed. Two wooden objects lie with their ends exposed in the center of the picture. Our flashlights revealed numerous other objects farther back, lying either on the surface or protruding through a layer of smooth dirt that had fallen from the ceiling over the centuries.

Carole Gardner

Plate 136

The second photograph of the chamber, taken just inside, reveals the sculptured back wall, part of the ceiling, and wooden objects in disarray on the floor. There was no sign that burrowing animals had been present, which might have accounted for the disorder. The objects appear to have been rudely tossed in at random with little regard for their well-being. Could this mean that there had been some urgency to hide the pieces and quickly seal and disguise the entrance? The ceiling of the chamber is about 5 feet below the surface of the plaza above. Although we found the 8 to 10 inches of dirt on the floor to be completely dry, there was ample evidence on the objects that water had penetrated the chamber.

A diagram shows the tunnel behind the kiva wall that originates in the chamber where the carved wooden objects were found, then moves diagonally over to the horizontal stone altar (see plate 129, page 197) and vertically to the surface. Although the tunnel probably was used to bring air into the kiva, it may also have served as a means for those inside to communicate with those outside.

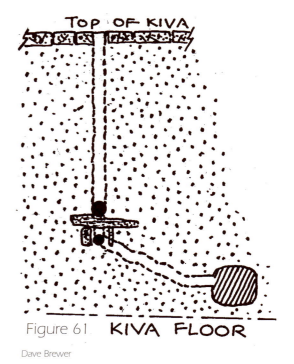

Figure 61 KIVA FLOOR

Dave Brewer

DANCE WANDS

Plate 137

This was our first good look at some of the sixty-three mysterious, carved wooden dance wands that were recovered from the secret chamber in the south wall of the kiva. Those artifacts that had been exposed to the air were generally in good condition, while others that were completely or partially buried by ceiling fall were mostly rotted. I constantly wonder if I am being too presumptuous in calling these objects dance wands. We actually have no idea what they are.

This was a hurried shot because my wife didn't much like the idea of having these things spread all over the dining room table.

Because these seventeen wooden artifacts were not covered by dirt in the storage chamber, they are in better condition than many of those that were covered. All have been carved from juniper, smoothed to a high polish, and then blackened by smoke, most of which easily could be removed by washing. The longest piece is 22 inches.

Plate 138

These eight carved juniper objects are some of the more exotic in the group of sixty-three that were found in the south chamber of the kiva. The second from the right is half a bow, but the use of the others cannot be determined. It appears to me that these pieces might have served some very highly specialized purpose that may have been known only to their maker.

Plate 139

This stretch of the geometric design was on the northwest wall of the kiva. No paint could be seen until the damp wall began to dry, which allowed thin layers of adobe to flake away exposing the various colors and designs. The best-case scenario would have been to carefully remove each of the 15 individual layers and record the images as they emerged. Unfortunately, that was not possible in this case because they dried too fast in the summer wind.

Plate 140

Five-inch geometric designs around the wall were periodically changed to scrolls. Occasionally 2½-inch-high, left-pointing red arrows were placed just above the white line seen here.

Plate 141

A red and white geometric design, which is 5 inches high, was painted 2 feet above the floor. It evidently circled the inside of the kiva, although we cannot be sure. Note the hole at top left that still contains the remnants of a wooden rod.

Plate 142

A jumble of a design found about 3 feet above the floor was made with selenite plaster paint. The soot-blackened wall of the kiva can be seen behind it. Similar markings were found on outer layers that fell away. Could this be ancestral puebloan writing? Note the geometric red designs at the lower right.

Plate 143

Plate 144

The four points of this morning star design are still under a few thin layers of adobe mud, some of which contain red and white geometric and scroll designs. Inside the 4-inch black circle are what appear to be two white eyes. It has been suggested that this image might represent some astronomical event. Other identical morning star images were discovered around the wall in different layers. Although all have now dried and fallen from the wall, samples of red, white, yellow, black, and green colors have been saved for analysis.

Carole Gardner

RED BIRD AND BONE

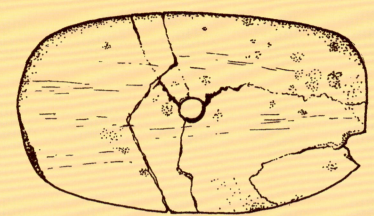

Figure 62

These two life-size drawings by Carole Gardner show the objects that were recovered from behind an adobe plug in the west wall of the kiva. The broken bird is made from unfired red clay. The bone object at left, which is 1/16-inch-thin, was probably carved from the scapula of a large animal.

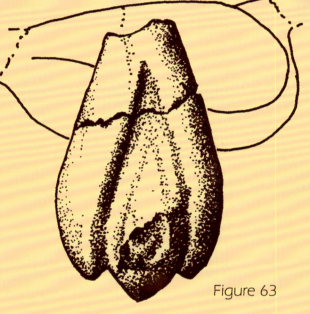

Figure 63

Plate 145

An unfired red clay bird with folded wings was missing its head and tail when we found it. I accidentally broke it during its removal. The poor thing deserves a better lot that it has received from the hands of humans.

INTERESTING OBSERVER

Plate 146

A collared lizard that lived near the kiva spent a lot of time watching us to see what we were doing. She fed on other lizards, bugs, small snakes, and some vegetation. When she got mad, she would throw her mouth open to show us the jagged teeth on her lower jaw. If further provoked, she would spread the collar on her neck really wide and hiss. But it was all a rude bluff, and in the end she would scurry away, only to return later to taunt us again. She loved to pose for Charmay, the kids thought she was fun, and Jann said she was a good omen. The truth is, she was.

THOUGHTS TO PONDER:

1. How was the inside wall of the kiva blackened with soot, and why?
2. Why were so many large rocks in the debris that filled the kiva?
3. Did the Spanish make the Indians cover the murals and stop using the kiva?
4. What do the murals and other painted designs mean?
5. What was the purpose of the carved wands and how were they used?
6. Why were the peach seeds in the secret chamber with the wands?

WHAT IS IT?

Plate 147

This little black critter, 4 3/4 inches long, was made from a soft piece of steatite, a variety of talc that is easy to carve. It was found, all alone, about 14 inches below the surface of an historic room in Building XV. Its bulbous eyes, pot belly, and long tail provide enough confusing information to make each of us think it was intended to be some other kind of creature. Ken Tankersley, a genius friend of mine, thinks it is a dragonfly, which makes sense, since the cute little insects were very special to the Tewa Indians, who used them routinely as painted designs on their pottery. For them, the dragonfly was a symbol of the Nepokwai'i kachina, which is a Kokopelli that will either seduce a young woman or make her a pair of bridal moccasins. The hump or winged back symbolizes that it is a friendly Kokopelli full of gifts.

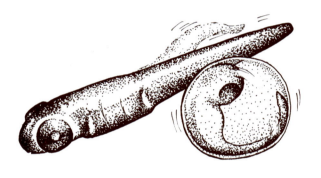

Archaeologist Ricky Lightfoot thinks it is a tadpole.

Figure 64

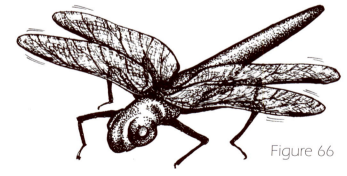

Figure 66

Charmay thinks it is a dragonfly.

I think it is a lizard. Please let me know what you think it is.
ffenn@earthlink.net

Figure 65

Drawings by Carole Gardner

CHICKEN

Figure 67

Sometimes I think that every person living at San Lazaro must have been an artist, or at least a craftsman. Maybe they had to be to survive. Why this appealing little chicken was molded out of clay is a mystery to us. Was it a fetish that had some magical power, or just a whimsical distraction that was formed around the evening campfire? In any event, its simplicity and graceful flowing lines make it something special. When I called it a chicken, Charmay jumped all over me, claiming that there is no way I could know what kind of bird it was. I gently reminded her that since I found the thing, I could call it whatever I wanted to. She had a smirk as she wandered off, but I know what she was thinking. Life-size drawing by Carole Gardner.

EL TORO

Plate 149

Plate 148

The three pictographs shown here were discovered in a small secluded rock shelter near the pueblo. Because the trees so thickly protect the shelter, we guessed that no other human eyes had seen this art in modern times.

The red painting depicts a Spanish bull with big horns being followed by two men. A four-legged animal is climbing the wooden staff being held by the man at right, who is wearing a large-brimmed hat.

Below the front legs of the bull is the faint image of the green-painted face of a kachina figure. The hand design was made by placing a hand tightly against the rock, then spewing a mouth full of white paint (probably selenite plaster) against it. When the hand, then covered with white paint, was removed, the blackness of the wall stood out in contrast to the white.

Carole Gardner

Plate 150

While pictographs are not unheard of in the Galisteo Basin, they certainly are rare, and rarer still are those showing birds. Four ravens resting on a corn stalk reside in the same little rock shelter with the red bull and human figures. This white painting is on the east wall in a naturally eroded alcove that is about 3 feet high.

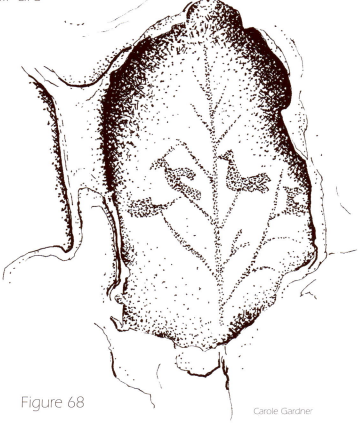

Figure 68

Carole Gardner

ANTLER MASK

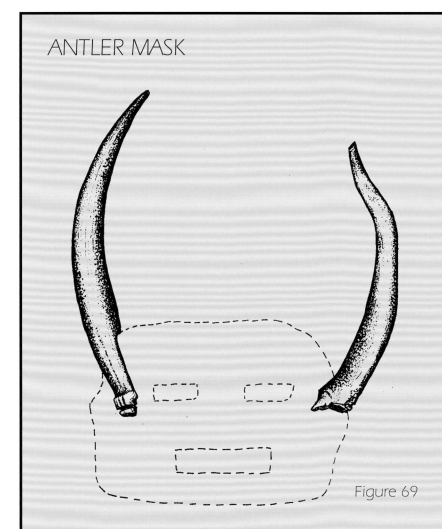

Figure 69

The remains of this mask, which has antler tines for horns, were found in Building XV. As it emerged under our trowels, it was easy to determine the entire outline of the object. Although the leather part between the horns had deteriorated to only a thick darkness in the dirt, still faintly visible were the rectangular eyes and mouth. A close study of the tine on the right revealed that it had been hacked with a metal blade. Unfortunately, the photos we took were too underexposed to use. The longest horn is 9 1/2 inches. Drawing by Carole Gardner.

FIBROLITE AXES

Plate 151

The beautiful axes illustrated here are made of fibrolite, which is a fibrous type of aluminum silicate mineral that was mined in the Truchas Peaks area of the Sangre de Cristo range northeast of Santa Fe. These axes were found in both the historic and prehistoric components of San Lazaro. The color of the stone varies from white to black and gray, to pinkish-red, brown, and variations of blue-green. It is not unusual to see a curious, slanted "X" scratched into the poll of an axe, as is visible on the black example in the upper right. Of the 66 stone axes and mauls that we have recovered at San Lazaro, about 20 percent are made of fibrolite. The largest axe in the picture is 5 1/2 inches.

STONE FEATHERS

Plate 152

These stone "feathers" were discovered about 10 inches above the floor of a room in Building XVI. The room was more than 7 feet deep, and thick layers of blown-in sand were both above and below the cache of feathers and other objects.

The feathers were resting one on top of the other in the remnants of a basket that appeared to have been made to hold the three objects. Fragments of the basket can still be seen adhering to the feather on the right, which is 13 inches long and made from a thin piece of slate with red ocher on both of its faces. Also in the basket, and packed in red ocher, were three thin, heavily worn, alibates jasper awls (see plate 153, next page). Apparently the basket containing the stone objects had been placed in a room that was ruined and had begun to fill, although the roof had not yet totally collapsed. The basket was covered with rocks and woody materials and evidently abandoned.

The center object made from translucent selenite has notches carved in its sides near a single hole. The third feather, on the left, shaped from an unknown soft stone, has ribs scratched on one side by a sharp tool and is highly polished, silky to the touch.

These special feathers were made by some long-forgotten Ancestral Puebloan, whose identity we will never know, to serve a unique purpose that likewise will forever remain a mystery to us. They were formed with a loving hand from fragile materials, yet they were deliberately secreted in a place where they would be safe for forty decades or more. We can only wonder what emotions shaped that person's deeds so long ago.

Carole Gardner

Plate 153

Three red alibates jasper awls, discovered nestled in a small cake of red ocher, evidently had been contained in a small leather bag before being placed in the basket beside the three stone feathers. The longest awl is 2 5/8 inches.

Figure 70

The stone feathers (see plate 152, page 218) were nestled in a cylindrical, plaited basket that appeared to have been made to order. This photograph shows a deteriorated fragment of the basket enlarged 340 percent. While the remains of the whole basket were there, only three small pieces could be recovered.

THOUGHTS TO PONDER:

1. Were the feathers tied to other objects as might be indicated by the holes and notches?
2. Did the Spanish, who suppressed the "pagan" rituals, influence the decision to hide the objects?
3. What role did the stone awls play, and what about the red ocher in which they were placed?

FLOOR POLISHERS

Plate 154

Floor polishers, which are just like pot smoothers only a lot larger, usually are made from basalt or diorite stones that range in size from 4 to 6 inches. These tools must have been highly prized after one or more of their faces became smooth and silky. In our excavations at San Lazaro, we have found that all of the adobe walls and floors had been hardened and highly polished from rubbing with these tools.

My old friend from Taos Pueblo, Joseph Sunhawk, who cut tepee poles for a living, said that when he had a muscle ache, his wife would heat a floor polisher in hot water and then "iron" the inflamed area to relieve the pain. How can you not like a guy that makes tepee poles for a living?

PREHISTORIC UNDER HISTORIC

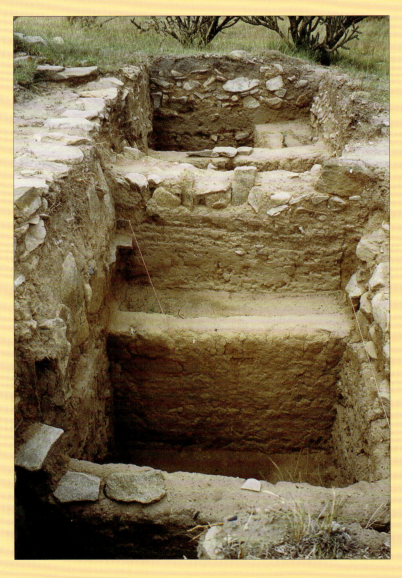

Plate 155

Historic stone walls on the north end of Building XV were built on top of prehistoric adobe rooms that may date as early as 1330. The lower rooms extend to the south the full length of the building and 80 feet beyond. More than 8 feet of dirt, sand, and debris had covered the earlier rooms, some of which are less than 25 square feet in size.

UNUSUAL SITUATIONS

Plate 156

A room on the north end of Building XV was constructed over a prehistoric trash mound that had been used and abandoned about 200 years earlier. The diagonal white lines in the bottom of the picture were made by ashes that had been unceremoniously dumped. The brown layer above the ashes is sand that had blown in and covered the trash mound after it fell into disuse about 1400. Those who erected the stone house above probably did not know they were building over a garbage dump.

This room in Building XV has a curious 8-inch-wide stone enclosure in the middle of the floor. No ashes or artifacts were found either in or around it. This feature is yet another of the many puzzles at San Lazaro that seem to have no modern day equivalent or explanation.

Plate 157

ALTAR IN THE HISTORIC PLAZA

Each summer archaeologist George Zeimens and his wife, Geri, bring teenagers to San Lazaro to camp and work at the pueblo. They are part of a group called Expanding Environments sponsored by the Western History Historic Preservation Association in Lingle, Wyoming. In 2000, twenty-three teenagers came as part of a nine-week archaeological endeavor.

One of their first projects was to excavate a curious and tantalizing mound in the historic plaza surrounded by Buildings XV and XVI, which were occupied during the first Spanish intrusion into New Mexico.

The rectangular mound was 5 feet wide and 11 feet long. Igneous rocks (latite) still were visible where they stood vertically to a depth of about 9 inches. Thus the original shape of this feature was obvious before its excavation began.

Plate 158

A professional documentary photographer videotapes the altar with some of the artifacts in situ, while teenage Wyoming excavators Keria Adams and Cailin Schamel supervise. Note the small two-handled jar in the flagstone box.

In his report, Zeimens said that the rectangular footing is aligned east-west, and that the north wall is aligned approximately 100 degrees west of magnetic north. He further stated:

> Several stones appeared to be in disarray within the confines of the rectangular feature, but as soon as some of the upper ones were removed, a deliberate structural pattern emerged. Three large, perpendicular slab stones protruded to the ground surface, with several pieces of volcanic cinder and petrified wood scattered in the vicinity. To the east, the top edges of 1/2-inch-thick, perpendicular, red flagstone slabs revealed a boxed rectangular vault filled with what appeared to be rubble of stones and dirt. The larger stones to the west were eventually found to construct a U-shaped enclosure, the opening of which faced nearly directly east toward the flagstone vault.

Once it was determined that the feature had probably been built upon the original ground surface, excavation of the rectangle's interior continued down to the level of the foundation wall. A large, egg-shaped stone approximately 8 by 10 inches with apparent spalling and a circular percussion indentation appeared at the opening of the U-shaped enclosure.

After the rubble stones and dirt were removed from the first few inches of the flagstone vault, the top of a small vessel appeared (see plate 158, previous page). It had been buried in the geometric center, with its two handles facing east-west. Opposite the handles a zigzag line of galena glaze paint extends from top to bottom on each side of the jar. Zeimens retrieved the dirt contents for later analysis.

It seems obvious that this whole feature is an altar that was constructed with great care, as demonstrated by the regularity of the foundation walls, the flagstone vault, and the U-shaped feature within the enclosure.

Although the associated medicine and small pottery bowl appear to have been strategically placed, the reasons for such action can only be conjecture at this late date.

Since the foundation walls are still standing in pristine condition and no rubble rocks were found around the periphery, is it possible that the walls were disassembled at Spanish insistence, and that the ceremonial assemblage was covered with dirt to disguise the feature's function as an altar?

The case also can be made that since the altar was covered with only a few inches of dirt when we found it, it could have been in use later than historic records might indicate. Could this be evidence that the buildings surrounding this feature remained occupied after the revolt of 1680, and that this altar was constructed so that the old religious practices could be continued?

Plate 159

In the historic plaza, Wyoming teenagers David Heitman and Mindy Schamel map and make notes about the altar and its mysteries. Behind the cholla cactus, up against Building XVI, the kiva waits to be discovered. In the left center of the picture (outside the altar wall), is a test pit we dug in search of the original plaza floor, which we found about 16 inches down. It would have been exciting to have seen the altar when it was new and being used.

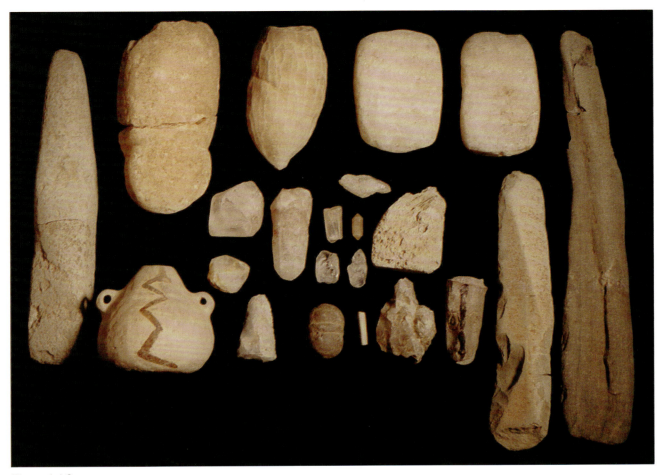

Plate 160

Artifacts recovered from the altar in the historic plaza include: three long, slender kiva bells and a stone phallus (top row, second from left), which were probably deliberately broken or "killed" before being placed in the altar. The small, handled jar in the bottom row at left was found in the center of a flagstone vault inside the altar. Other objects in the picture are quartz crystals, a piece of volcanic pumice, a pair of lightning stones, a concretion, and a pottery snake figure. The kiva bell at left is just over 9 inches long.

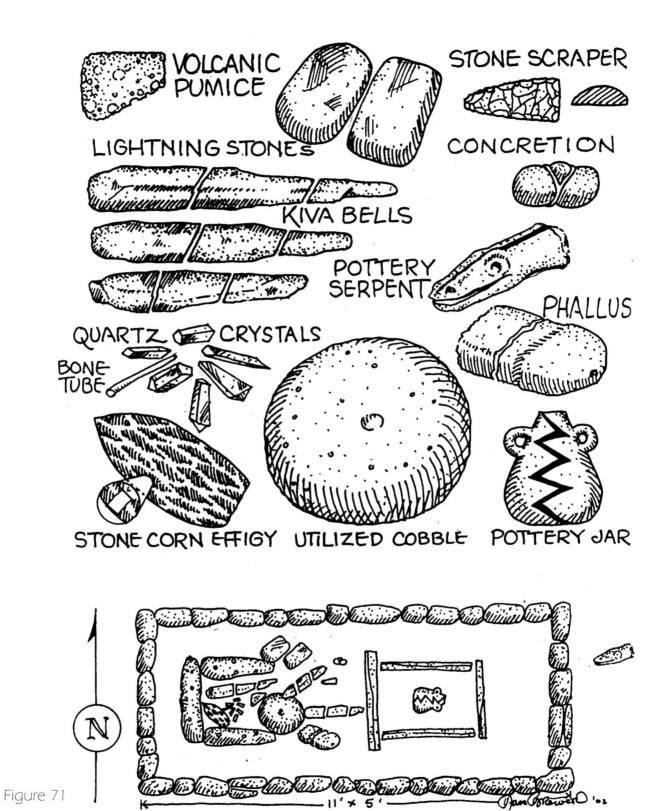

Figure 71

Dave Brewer made this drawing of the altar and its associated artifacts.

CORN EFFIGY

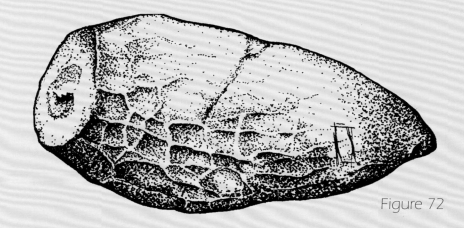

Figure 72

A life-size drawing by Carole Gardner depicts a corn effigy that was recovered from the altar in the historic plaza. In his report, George Zeimens described it as follows:

> Near the top of the flagstone vault, lying near the southwest corner, a tapered, conical concretion 4 1/2 inches long and 2 1/4 inches in diameter, of the type commonly called "turtle rock," was discovered. One end of the stone had been fractured off, and the facets sunken into the stone lent the appearance suggestive of an ear of maize (corn). Near the conical tip, the stone has been incised with a series of lines forming a small rectangle that is the same shape as the large feature being excavated.

Carole Gardner

Plate 161

A stone phallus made from a crystalline material was found in two pieces in close proximity to each other in the altar. The two sections appear to have been deliberately broken apart, and heavy wear patterns can be seen on most of its faces.

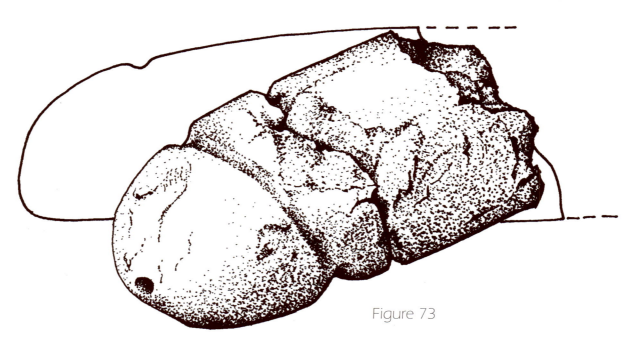

Figure 73

This life-size drawing by Carole Gardner shows the phallus after the two pieces were rejoined at its midsection. Most of the damage is to the top of the object, which is flat on the bottom.

Figure 74

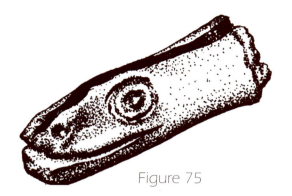

Figure 75

A pottery fragment that appears to be the head of a snake or lizard was discovered a few inches east of the altar in the historic plaza. It may represent Quetzalcoatl, a mythical figure that appears frequently in ancient Aztec artifacts. Similar figures called plumed serpents are found in rock art all across the Southwest, but this is the first such figure we have seen at San Lazaro. It was almost surely detached from some other object, such as a ladle. Life-size drawing by Carole Gardner.

POINTS TO PONDER:

1. Why is there a foundation to what must have been a small room, but no evidence of walls?
2. Why were some of the ceremonial objects deliberately broken?
3. What purpose did the small pottery canteen serve, and why was it hidden near the bottom of the flagstone vault?
4. What was the purpose of the U-shaped feature?

METATES AND MANOS

These metates, manos, choppers and hammers are a few of those recovered from rooms in Buildings XV and XVI. Metate is a Spanish word for a stone with a flat or concave surface on which grain, nuts, etc., can be ground by a smaller stone called a muller or mano. One fact that strongly supports the belief that corn was the primary food source for the Indians at San Lazaro is the great abundance of metates that have been recovered. Usually there are four or more in the collapsed debris of an average room. Since metates are rarely found on the floor, most of the kitchen duties must have been performed on the roof.

Plate 162

The process of preparing dried corn to eat began when kernels were placed on a metate that had a coarse surface. As the mano was moved back and forth across the metate, the kernels were crushed into fragments. Metates and manos with smoother surfaces may have then been used to reduce the fragments into

corn meal or even powder, depending on what the recipe required.

The more grinding that was done, the smoother the tools became, which greatly reduced their effectiveness in grabbing whole kernels and crushing them. The easiest solution was to "sharpen" the metates and manos by pecking their grinding surfaces with a sharp, pointed chopper, thus making them rough again, a process that was much faster than starting from scratch to make new tools. However, quite often the grinders were broken in the pecking process. Many broken and derelict metates and manos are sprinkled around the pueblo where they now serve as habitats for different colors of lichen.

Metates and manos have been found much less frequently in Buildings I and II on the prehistoric side across the arroyo. One reason may be that fewer people were in residence during the years those rooms were occupied. Because the volume of processed bones recovered from those rooms also was much less, apparently the abundance of food at San Lazaro was much greater after the Spanish arrived.

Carole Gardner

ALIBATES SCRAPERS

Plate 163

Alibates jasper occurs in dolomite outcroppings within a 10-mile area around Lake Meredith along the Canadian River brakes north of Amarillo, Texas. Although the stone occurs in many colors, the distinctive red is the most prominent. The Texas quarries have been mined for more than 12,000 years, and some of the flint made its way into New Mexico.

At San Lazaro, the stone apparently was very much revered because it was used only for making tools that required sharp and lasting edges such as scrapers and drills. Of the hundreds of arrowheads found in our excavations, only one is made of alibates. We think the stone was so cherished that it was used to make tools that a person could keep and use over and over. Forty-one scrapers and fifteen drills made from the stone are in our collections. A flaked alibates animal fetish was discovered in the medicine assemblage related to the prehistoric masks found in Building I. This photograph shows some of the scrapers which were used to remove flesh from fresh animal skins.

STONE DRILLS

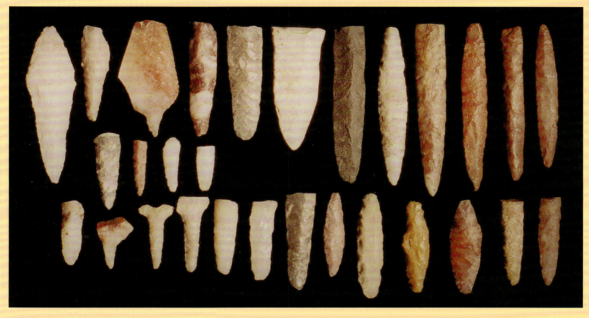

Plate 164

Most of the stone drills pictured have been heavily used, which has dulled their edges. About 40 percent of those found at San Lazaro are made from alibates jasper.

THE SAN LAZARO CHARTER

The pueblo and its associated properties are owned by the San Lazaro Corporation, whose officers recognize their responsibilities as guardians and protectors of the site. The great abundance of pottery fragments, stone hammers, choppers, flaked stone tools, animal bones, and metates that cover the immediate landscape are a testimonial to that stewardship. We feel a strong obligation to maintain the artifacts as a collection, so none of them will ever be sold or bartered. We call the collection our own, and it is, but we also know that we are only temporary custodians of these artifacts that are of great historical importance. Although we are not young enough to know everything, we are doing our best.

POT POLISHERS

Plate 165

These little polishing stones, unmodified except by use, are some of my favorite artifacts. They are usually no larger than 2 inches and may have as many as three smoothing surfaces, which are usually flat or slightly convex. Because many of them have wear patterns that can be obtained only from polishing hundreds of pots, they were probably highly prized and handed down through the family.

Eric Blinman, who is an authority on prehistoric pot making, explained the process this way:

> **Burnishing usually starts while the body of the vessel is still pliable, refining the surface for either the addition of a slip or simply starting the process of achieving a polish. The exact timing depends on the clay being used. Sometimes there is a very narrow window of dryness when the clay doesn't stick too badly to the stone, but when the surface can be effectively smoothed and compacted. If burnishing is stopped too soon, many types of clay will go matte as they dry and continue to shrink, disrupting whatever lustrous surface has been produced to that point. Some clays can't be burnished after a certain point with-**

out risking damage to the surface. Modern Tewa tradition includes slip application to a dry pot, followed immediately by polishing as the slip dries out almost instantly.

The purposes of burnishing are to create a smoother and more lustrous surface as a background for the design, to make the surface less porous—more non-stick and easier to clean—and to make the surface harder, although in that regard firing temperature is more important.

GAMING PIECES

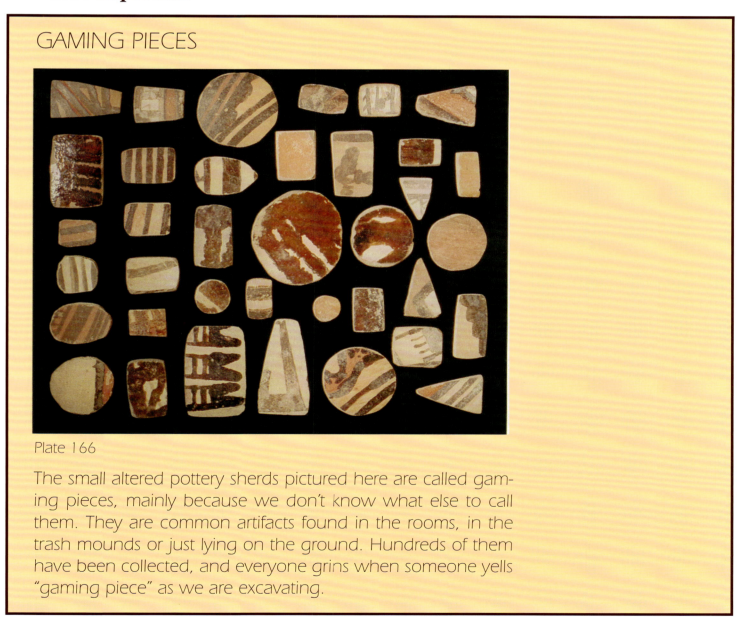

Plate 166

The small altered pottery sherds pictured here are called gaming pieces, mainly because we don't know what else to call them. They are common artifacts found in the rooms, in the trash mounds or just lying on the ground. Hundreds of them have been collected, and everyone grins when someone yells "gaming piece" as we are excavating.

ARROW SHAFT SMOOTHER

Plate 167

This 2 3/4-by-3-inch shaft smoother made from black schist is one of about thirty that have been unearthed in our work at San Lazaro. The groove near the top was used as an abrader to knock the rough edges off of an arrow shaft. Although this style of tool is not uncommon, no one has yet learned what either the vertical ridge at bottom left or the drilled hole, which is almost 1 inch deep, was used for.

SELENITE ARTIFACTS

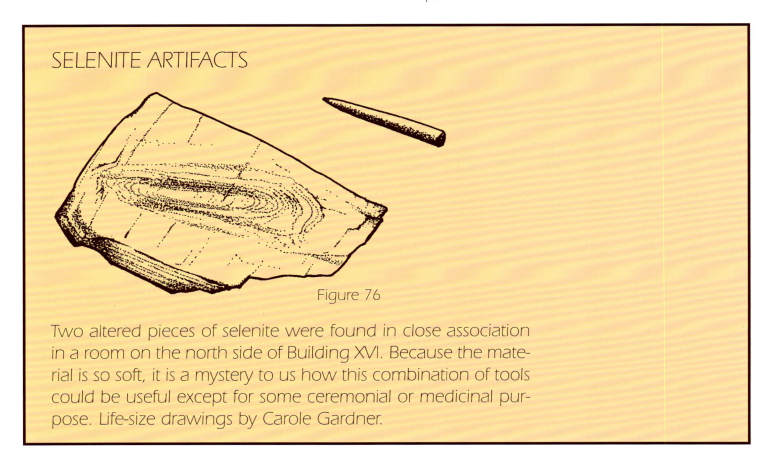

Figure 76

Two altered pieces of selenite were found in close association in a room on the north side of Building XVI. Because the material is so soft, it is a mystery to us how this combination of tools could be useful except for some ceremonial or medicinal purpose. Life-size drawings by Carole Gardner.

GLASS BEADS

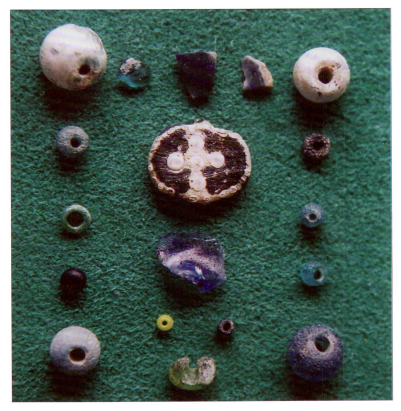

Plate 168

These are all of the glass beads that we have recovered at San Lazaro. The two small seed beads, near the bottom center, were found in an anthill near Building XVI. All of the others were recovered from screened, excavated dirt, except for the largest one in the center, which is 7/16 of an inch long. It was picked up on the surface and may have been part of a rosary. These beads, all of which were made in Venice in the seventeenth century, were brought to the pueblo by the Spanish.

MAJOLICA AND PORCELAIN

Plate 169

The majolica fragments in the grouping at the top of this photo are parts of vessels imported to San Lazaro from Spain and Mexico in the seventeenth century. The different types represented include Aucilla style, Puebla Blue-on-white and

Puebla Polychrome. Four of the sherds that have holes drilled in them probably were used as spindle whorls. The round whorl in the center, which is 2 1/2 inches wide, was found on the floor of an 8-foot-deep room in Building XVII. Most of the other pieces were picked up in the trash mound to the south and west of the historic buildings.

The three fragments in the center are glass, which is very rare at the pueblo. As a matter of fact, these are three of only four pieces that we have found. Their appearance has been significantly altered by being in the ground for a few hundred years. They can appear almost phosphorescent when the sun strikes them just right.

The twenty-six pieces in the bottom row are Ming Dynasty porcelain from China. After the Spanish colonized the Philippines in 1565, they started importing goods from the Orient to Manila, where they were put on Spanish galleons bound for Acapulco. They were then loaded on mule trains for the 225-mile trip to Mexico City. Porcelain is very heavy, so that trip must have been pretty hard on the mules. In Mexico City, the Spanish explorers, merchants, homesteaders, and traders again loaded the mules for the long trip to San Lazaro, which is over 1,200 miles as the crow flies. The large piece (3 inches wide) in the center of the photo was picked up on the surface. We think it is part of a lid to a storage container.

SPINDLE WHORLS

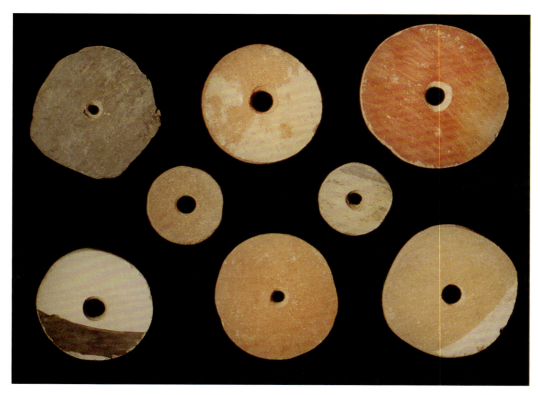

Plate 170

About fifty spindle whorls and their fragments have been recovered in our excavations at San Lazaro in both prehistoric and historic contexts. Most of them were made from broken pieces of pottery, but other materials that were used as well include sandstone, Spanish majolica, and Ming Dynasty Chinese porcelain. We are sure that many whorls also were made of wood, but those have long ago decayed along with most of the other perishable tools and garments that were commonly used at the pueblo. One fragment of a scorched cotton weaving was recovered in Building II, which was occupied before 1520.

Although archaeological investigations to date have not indicated that the inhabitants of San Lazaro raised cotton, the evidence of numerous spindle whorls has led us to believe they did. In any event, cotton surely was available to weavers in prehistoric times.

ANTELOPE CARVED IN STONE

Figure 77

We were lucky to have noticed this carving on a 5 1/2-inch piece of feldspar as we discarded rocks from our excavation in Building XV. Because it appears to be unique in Southwestern archaeology, we think it might have been made by a Spaniard.

Carole Gardner

WOOLEN EMBROIDERY

Plate 171

Laurie Webster, an expert on early Southwestern textiles, studied the fragments pictured here and described them as the remains of woolen embroidery yarns that were formerly applied to a cotton garment, probably a kilt, breechcloth, or manta. The textile probably was embroidered sometime between 1613 and 1700. The yarns are made of the Spanish-introduced fiber, sheep wool, and are 2-ply, z-spun, S-twist. The largest piece, which consists of parallel rows of yarns worked in a running-stitch embroidery technique, appears to be the remains of a band or border with a diagonally cross-hatched diamond design. Webster said the samples also include numerous strands of coiled woolen yarns ranging from 0.4-0.8cm in diameter, one of which has three, 1cm-high triangles spaced 2cm apart. These fragments probably represent the remains of a decorative border that was applied to the edges of the garment with an overcast stitch.

Also present is a strand of yarn tied in a series of overhand knots, possibly the remains of a tassel.

Another fragment of yarn that was recovered from the crease of the embroidery sample was examined by Webster under 100x magnification and tentatively identified as cotton. This finding suggests that the woolen embroidery originally had been applied to a cotton garment, which had long since deteriorated. Wool preserves better than cotton under most archaeological conditions. Similar examples of woolen embroidery lacking remnants of the original cotton fabric to which they had been applied were identified by Webster in post-contact assemblages from Awatovi (Hopi), Hawikuh (Zuni), Giusewa and Unshagi (Jemez), and Pecos. The San Lazaro samples were discovered together on the floor of a room in Building XV.

Textiles usually don't last very long buried in the ground, so we feel fortunate to have recovered these two pieces. The one at left is made of carbonized, handspun, plain-weave, native cotton that is embellished with three, and possibly four, rows of twined-stitch embroidery that was used to decorate and reinforce the fabric. It may have been part of a blanket or other garment and dates to ca.1400.

The fragment at right, one of thirteen pieces that were found together, dates between 1540 and 1680. It is woven from natural sheep wool, and is probably the remains of a blanket or manta.

Both fragments, identified by Laurie Webster, are magnified about 40 percent.

Plate 172

THIRTEEN POTS

Plate 173

The ten small vessels pictured here were recovered from an inside room near the plaza in Building XV. They were clustered together about 14 inches below the ground surface, along with three larger bowls and three terraced phyllite cloud figures (see plate 177, page 248). This cache may have been deliberately secreted in the falling-down rubble of the room.

Only one of these vessels (the largest is 3 inches tall) lacks a galena glaze design, and none of them show any use or wear patterns. Zuni archaeologist Ed Ladd thought they were used to carry sacred water from the spring for the medicine ceremonies.

In excavations at Pecos Pueblo (1915-1925) supervised by A. V. Kidder, about forty "little containers," similar to those pictured, were recovered. In his book, <u>The Pottery of Pecos</u>, Kidder states that these are vessels " . . . whose specialized shape and decoration indicate that they are not ordinary household utensils. The places in which they were found, as well as the objects which accompanied some of them, render it certain that they were made and used for cult purposes."

In 1912, at Pueblo Blanco, also in the Galisteo Basin, Nels Nelson excavated a room that contained a "stone idol" similar to the one he recovered in Building VI at

San Lazaro (see plate 37, page 68), along with concretions and eight small vessels like those described here. Nearly all of those found are small and possess two handles, as if they were designed to be suspended.

An early Glaze Period D (1490-1520) bowl was found with a cache of twelve other vessels and three slate cloud terrace figures. It is 8 inches wide, 5 1/2 inches tall, measures 6 inches at the mouth, and has a slight scraped wear pattern on the bottom.

Plate 174

This charming tiny jar, which is just 2 7/8 inches wide, has faces painted on each side. The face you see here is that of a married woman, and on the other side is the face of a single woman with a butterfly hairdo (see jar 185, page 321). At least that is what Ed Ladd thought. It was found in a cache with thirteen other pots and three slate cloud terrace figures.

Plate 175

Carole Gardner

247

Plate 176

This terraced bowl measures 8 1/2 inches by 7 3/4 inches and is 4 1/2 inches tall. It is not well made, being somewhat asymmetrical and awkward looking, and the glaze paint designs are a total bafflement to me. It was found in five pieces with the cache of other pots (see plate 173) and shows no wear on the bottom. It has what appears to be a cross more than an inch high painted on the inside of one of the terraces, a design that Ladd said probably is a star. He also thought the whole cache of pots and slate objects was personal family medicine.

Plate 177

Three terraced stone objects were discovered stacked one on top of the other in close proximity to the cache of small pottery vessels. The thickest part of any of the three is 5/16 of an inch, and the average thickness is about 1/4 of an inch. The largest is 11 inches tall, 8 inches wide, and has a hole that was drilled from both sides. The figures, which are made of phyllite, a dark, salty-gray, micaceous metamorphic rock whose parent is slate, were shaped by percussion flaking with a billet. Most of the edges are ground smooth. Ed Ladd thought they were used as kiva bells and that, when in use, the small end pointed down.

Terraced figures are a familiar design in the Southwest. Of the thirteen vessels found in this assemblage, nine of them exhibit a terraced pattern of some sort. An old friend from Taos Pueblo said the figures are stair steps to the clouds.

Plate 178

This Glaze Period E (1515-1650) shouldered bowl, measuring 7 1/2 inches wide and 2 1/2 inches tall, has a four-legged animal standing on the left rim, whose head and tail are missing. On the opposite rim, a damaged area provided evidence that another figure had once been present. Four years after the bowl had been recovered, on the surface I found a small pottery bird of identical coloring with its wings spread. It exactly fit the damaged spot, so I glued it back in place on its perch. The little bird had somehow managed to move 300 feet away from where the bowl had been buried more than 320 years earlier. I think they are happy to be reunited.

AVIAN DESIGNS

Plate 179

Nearly all of the painted pottery vessels that we recovered at San Lazaro contain some kind of bird design, usually that of a macaw or a parrot. Often the designs are so abstract that my six-year-old granddaughter, Noah, has been called to come in to identify what the ancient potter had in mind. Of course, she always has an answer for us. I think she is going to be an archaeologist.

This photo shows some of the many such designs we have found.

FEATHER HAIRPIECE

In a prehistoric room below Building XV, which is historic, we found this 7-inch bowl fragment. The face is reminiscent of others that have been found at San Lazaro in both historic and prehistoric contexts. Jan Orcutt thinks it could date before 1350.

Figure 78

VIGAS

The remnants of vigas and latillas made of juniper rest where they fell in a partially filled room on the south plaza side of Building XVI. Because juniper is a very hard wood, it rots more slowly than piñon or ponderosa, all three of which grow in the immediate area.

Plate 180

PUKIS

Most of the larger bowls and ollas constructed at San Lazaro must have been formed with the use of a puki, which is a mold or turntable on which new pottery vessels were formed. In the small sampling of rooms we excavated, the 26 pukis recovered ranged from 6 1/2 to 15 1/2 inches in diameter.

Plate 181

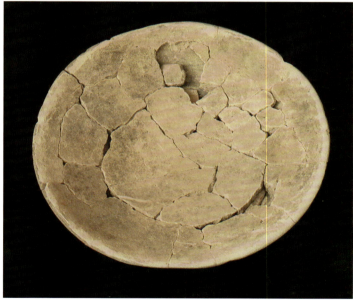

Plate 182

The puki illustrated here, which was found in Building I, is made from a San Lazaro Polychrome olla that dates to about 1450. The top of the olla was somehow separated from its base, a 10-inch piece of which was then placed in the inverted top portion of the olla, closing the orifice or neck.

Puki linings were prepared with selenite plaster with maybe a few wood ashes thrown in. The fairly thick mixture was applied to the inside of the bowl where some of it seeped under the basal sherd sealing it tight and caulking the two pieces into one. The puki pictured in plates 181 and 182 has fill that is more than an inch thick in the bottom, but tapers up to a thin edge at the rim.

After the plaster mix set chemically, it provided a surprisingly stable foundation that the potter could comfortably use as a base on which to spin the coils of subsequent bowls.

The circular base of this puki is ground uniformly level, probably by moving it back and forth on a flat piece of sandstone. Such a level base was necessary to keep the puki from tilting when it was placed on the ground. The same evidence of base-grinding appears on every puki we examined that had been made from an olla. The specimen pictured is 3 1/4 inches high and 12 1/2 inches in diameter.

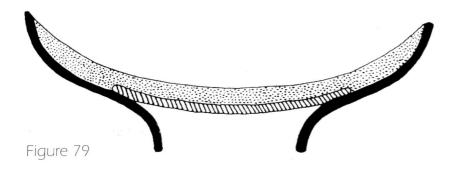

Figure 79

This illustration is a diagrammatic cross section of the puki seen in plates 181 and 182. The black outer line is the upper neck and shoulder of what was originally a pottery olla. The striped area is the sherd that was used to close the neck. The spotted area is a hardened plaster mixture used as a base on which a pot is formed. Drawing by the author.

POTTERY WORKSHOP

Plate 183

The first of three rooms that we excavated in Building IX was occupied for 30 years or so starting about 1300. Evidently it was a place where pottery was manufactured, because many of the objects in the room were used in that process. In the top center of the photo are two carefully placed pukis stacked one on top of the other. In the left center, against the wall, is another one made from the top half of a San Lazaro Polychrome olla that measures about 15 inches across. Two crushed bowls can be seen near the top corners of the room. In addition to the 11 manos that remain on the floor where they were discovered are a basalt floor polisher, five pottery smoothers, a bone awl, chunks of red and yellow ocher, and a ball of wet clay.

It is easy to imagine the bustle of activity and movement of human bodies that took place in and around this room almost 700 years ago.

FLORAL COLORS

The cane cholla cactus blooms in warm weather only if its roots can get enough moisture in the spring. Otherwise, their numerous spiky arms will be devoid of brilliant color. Small rodents bring the seeds home and store them in nests under the rocks from which the rooms are built. A season later this prolific plant seems to be growing everywhere.

Plate 184

If the summer monsoon rains arrive at San Lazaro early enough in the season, the ground can become wildly ablaze with a broad expanse of colors—reds, whites, yellows, greens, browns, purples, and more. Because the sandy soil is generally poor, one must admire the abundance of tiny flowers in a landscape that is usually sparse and lonesome looking. The 1/2-inch blooms of many different perennials, such as the small daisy-like (originally called the eye-of-the-day or day's eye) plants, hold on tenaciously against the assaults of hard-blowing winds and chewing animals, only to die when the temperature drops, as winter weather descends. The only living colors then are the greens of the piñons, ponderosas, and junipers, the browns of dormant grasses and bushes, and the beautiful, multi-colored lichens, which are always there no matter what.

Barton Wright

BONE ORNAMENT

Plate 185

Wear and polish between the holes of this bone object prove that it was sewn onto something, probably for decoration, because its 3/32-inch thinness makes it too fragile to be used as a button. If it did not have the distinctive wear pattern we would call it a whizzer. It is 2 inches wide and was found in Building XV.

REPORTING OUR WORK

When we first started working at San Lazaro over twenty years ago, with a labor force that was rarely more than family and close friends, our focus was on Buildings I and II, where we excavated thirty-five rooms, about half of the dwellings in those roomblocks. When we felt satisfied that our knowledge was adequate to describe the early life of those people, we moved across the creek into the historic buildings where we hoped to learn more about how early Spanish colonizers had influenced the native population.

We quickly learned that long hours of tedious, dirty, sweaty, apparently fruitless work would nearly always be punctuated by moments of extreme excitement as some special object or bit of information presented itself to us in a split-second of euphoric surprise. In a collective effort to share and savor every morsel of information, we have saved everything, including sheep droppings, burned latillas, horse hooves and small utilized obsidian flakes, of which we have more than 3,600. Although our efforts have been difficult at times, and our hours long, we have not excavated even one percent of the rooms in the pueblo.

Our mission never has been diluted, so when someone in our crew has yelled, "Quick, come see," we all have dropped what we were doing and run. It seems that everyone was taking copious photographs along the way to document our work, so we now have thousands.

Our hope is that a millennium from now, when the last secret of San Lazaro has been revealed and its final mystery has been solved, our work will still be considered important.

CATAPULT BALLS

Although the history books do not say that Coronado and his army visited San Lazaro Pueblo, and while we may never know if they did or not, there are clues that can influence our thinking.

Pedro de Castañeda, the most reliable chronicler of the Coronado expedition into New Mexico in 1540, made an interesting observation. When describing villages that the 29-year-old Coronado and his army had seen, he wrote:

> There is a village, small and strong, between Cicuye (Pecos) and the province of Quirex (pueblos on the Rio Grande west of San Lazaro), which the Spaniards named Ximena, and another village almost deserted, only one part of which is inhabited. This was a large village, and judging from its condition and newness, it appeared to have been destroyed. They call this the village of the granaries or silos, because large underground cellars were found here stored with corn. There was another large village farther on, entirely destroyed and pulled down, in the yards of which there were many stone balls, as big as 12-quart bowls, which seem to have been thrown by engines or catapults, which have destroyed the village.

Could San Lazaro be the village that Castañeda had described as being destroyed by catapult balls?

One Spanish soldier who wrote home said that the pueblo on the west side of Del Chorro Creek was "almost abandoned," a comment that would fit Castañeda's description. Could concretions that are naturally formed in sandstone have been confused with the stone balls that Coronado's army saw, to which Castañeda referred? Many such balls can still be seen in some abundance around the pueblo, especially east of Building XVI, where hundreds rest on the ground as the sandstone has decomposed from around them. In these pictures, it appears that stone balls had been catapulted into the sandstone.

Plate 186

Plate 187

MISCELLANEOUS ARROWHEADS

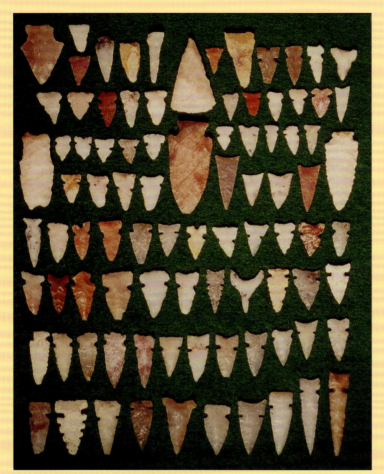

Plate 188

Barton Wright

Although more than half of the 589 arrowheads in our San Lazaro collection were made from obsidian, many other types of stone also were used including alibates jasper, Pedernal agate, Edwards Plateau chert, phosphoria, petrified wood, flattop chert, basalt, siltstone and different kinds of chalcedony.

Occasionally a point is uncovered by our trowels, but the vast majority are found lying on the ground after a rain or a wind storm. Although the small arrowheads are often called "bird points," they also were used to kill large animals such as buffalo and elk.

OBSIDIAN ARROWHEADS

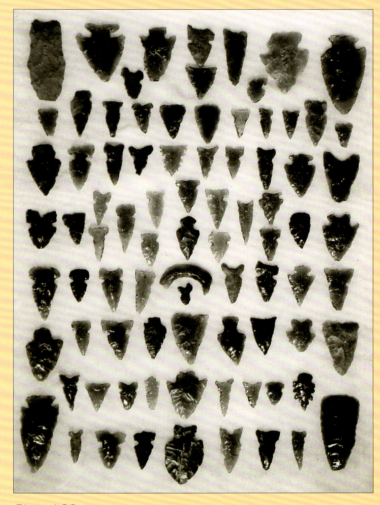

Plate 189

Obsidian, a type of glass produced by volcanic action, comes from a number of sources in New Mexico, the largest being in the Jemez Mountains near Los Alamos. It was the preferred material for making arrowheads because it was readily available, easy to flake, and produced sharp edges.

PROBLEMATICALS

Plate 190

Stones such as these that have been shaped for some special reason are frequently found at San Lazaro. Most of the time they have similar indentations on both sides, and no one seems to know what purpose they serve. Guesses range from bases on which loom poles rested, to mortars where piñon nuts were cracked. Some might think they were used as a device in which to mix pigments, but they are too small for that and besides, we have not seen color in any of them. The one in the top center of the photo is different in that it is conical shaped with a pointed bottom.

AGATE TALISMAN

Plate 191

Beautiful stones are appreciated by all peoples, and the San Lazaro natives were not exceptions. This ground and polished piece of agate was found in a trash mound where it was probably placed as an offering. It is shown slightly larger than life size.

RED AND GREEN STONES

Plate 192

Painted rocks are extremely rare at San Lazaro so these two are the first we have seen besides two that were in the mask assemblage. The red color is hematite that contains minute particles of mica that sparkle in the sun. The green color was made from chrysocolla. The backs of both stones are red, and the longest one is 4 1/2 inches. They were found in a room on the north end of Building I.

STILT

Plate 193

After about 1300, lead ore, called galena, was mined locally and ground into powder on stone palettes. When mixed with water, the powder was applied as a glaze paint that was popular with the Indian potters at San Lazaro. After a vessel was painted, it was inverted and placed on stilts so that some air might be present in the firing process to provide an oxidizing atmosphere, which kept unwanted black smudge clouds from ruining the potter's designs. Although lead melts at a relatively high temperature compared with other pottery paints, in many cases the galena paint would melt and run off the vessel and onto the stilt, as seen in this photo.

Pottery firing areas have been located both on the southwestern periphery of San Lazaro and in the historic plaza, where we found several stilts still in place, deeply surrounded by charcoal and ashes.

ARMS AND SPIDERS

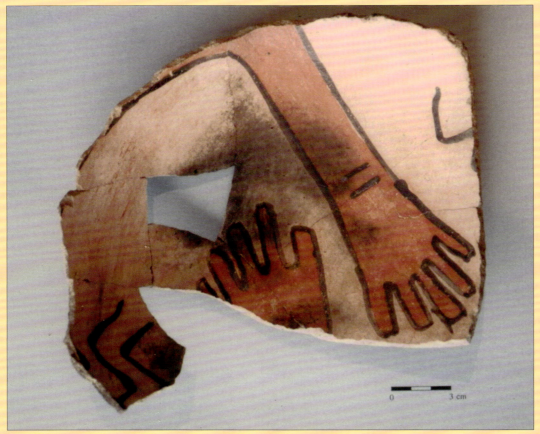

Plate 194

Rarely are bowls with human figures found at San Lazaro, and this is all we were able to recover of one. The arm is either tattooed or is wearing make-believe bracelets. The long legs on both sides of the arms could belong to tarantulas, which can be seen walking around the pueblo during certain times of the year. We have not seen spiders painted on local pottery before.

BROKEN BOWLS

Plate 195

Plate 196

Large bowls and jars are nearly always broken when we find them. If they were abandoned on the roof of a room, they were usually broken years later when the roof collapsed and they went tumbling in along with timbers and large rocks. Likewise, if they were left on the floor, they were hit by falling debris. The large olla in the top photo had been on the roof, and the plain ware jar in the bottom photo still rests in the corner of a room where we found it, with a mano at its side.

DRILLED HOLES

Plate 197

Modern potters who study the ancient ways of making pottery say that it takes at least thirty man-hours to produce an olla or bowl if you copy the old styles and methods of manufacture. For that reason, the San Lazaro potters must have taken inordinate steps to protect their pottery. When a hairline crack appeared in the side of a vessel, the procedure was to drill holes on each side of the crack and apply a tie-wrap between the holes, thus preventing the crack from widening. I have seen as many as twelve holes for ties on one pot. This photo shows a few of the many sherds that have turned up in our excavations that have such holes.

SUNSET

Plate 198

Someone once said that no sunset is prettiest in only one place, and that is probably true. This sunset, taken through the cane cholla on top of Roomblock VII, is one of Charmay's best because it captures a romantic mood that must have been felt many times by the San Lazaro villagers. It is difficult to imagine the savagery of an enemy raiding party or the cries of a hungry child at this time of day.

REVERIE

When I was just a kid, more than sixty-five years ago, my father and I often walked the wooded hills and along the creek bottoms in Texas, searching for signs of ancient man. We loved doing that together. The thrill of finding my first arrowhead ranks among my fondest memories. It was not the arrowhead alone that marked the event; it was also that my father was there to share it with me. I have long remembered the expression of satisfaction on his face as he watched mine. A few years before he died, he sent me this poem. Some words can be worth a thousand pictures.

Plate 199

O'er fields of new turned sod
Communing with my God,
I tramped alone.

And in a furrow bed
I found an arrowhead
Chiseled from stone.

Then fancy fled on wings
Back to primeval things
Seeking the light.

What warrior drew the bow,
Sighted and let it go
On its last flight?

How oft this flinten head
On deadly errand sped
I do not know

Nor will the silent flint
Reveal the slightest hint
How long ago.

Were its grim story told
What tales would it unfold,
Tales that would chill!

I know but this one thing
Beyond all questioning,
'Twas meant to kill.

Ages have worn away,
Warriors have gone their way,
Their bones are dust.

Proof of a craftsman's skill
Survives the ages still
Left in my trust.

Anon

PONDERING

Plate 200

Forrest strikes his usual summer pose as he closely supervises the excavations in Building XV.

THE COLORED POTTERY OF SAN LAZARO PUEBLO

FRANCIS HARLOW AND DWIGHT LANMON

Plate 201

Plate 202

Although the styles of pueblo Indian pottery tend to vary slowly in time, they often differ substantially from one set of villages to another. Rio Grande Glaze Ware refers to one of these general styles. Vessels of this category were made during the period from ca.1300 until ca.1700 in the villages lying principally between modern Santa Fe to the north and Albuquerque to the south, and between Zia Pueblo to the west and Pecos Pueblo to the east. Tewa Matte-Paint Ware is another broad category of pottery made in the Tewa villages north of Santa Fe, including Tesuque and San Ildefonso.

Vessels of these two wares differ greatly from each other, especially in the materials used for building each vessel and the pigments used for painting the designs. Often the designs themselves differ considerably from one ware to another.

San Lazaro Pueblo is situated near the middle of the Rio Grande Glaze Ware area, and its ceramics are typical of that ware. Although the styles have been studied extensively, only occasionally has there been the abundance of material that has come from San Lazaro. A detailed study of this material would be rewarding, but such an analysis is beyond the scope and intent of this book. Instead, we present numerous photos that illustrate the skill and artistry of the San Lazaro people making pottery of great serviceability and beauty, together with a brief text that discusses some of the salient features.

Glaze Painted Pottery from San Lazaro Pueblo

The pottery from San Lazaro Pueblo furnishes useful clues regarding the dates of occupation of the village. The evolution of styles, especially of vessel forms, follows closely the sequence that occurs at many of the middle Rio Grande pueblos. In some of these occurrences, the distinctive features, especially the rims of bowls, have been dated in a manner that shows considerable consistency from one village to another. Thus the presence of each style at San

Lazaro strongly indicates the time of manufacture, and thus of occupancy, even in the absence of primary dating evidence, such as the dendrochronology technique that has been confidently established for the region.

The conclusion from examination of numerous fragmentary and restorable vessels is that the occupation of San Lazaro commenced in the first half of the 1300s, expanded during the 1400s, and ended shortly after 1500. Later, from around 1600 until perhaps as late as 1680, there was a reoccupation of parts of the village. Thereafter, San Lazaro has been completely without inhabitants.

Virtually all of the decorated pottery made at San Lazaro was painted before firing with an emulsion of finely powdered lead oxide for the darker design lines, and often with a slip that fired to a red color. Sometimes the slip was applied over large areas of the pot, and sometimes it was applied only to the areas that would be outlined with the darker lead oxide pigment.

The appeal of lead oxide comes from the fact that the potters were able to achieve firing temperatures great enough (above about 880 degrees C) to melt the mineral and fuse the grains of powder so that they would solidify to a lustrous, glossy finish. The disadvantage of this material comes from its tendency to run, producing some irregularity in the decorative lines and occasionally resulting in obliteration of the artistic intentions of the potter. An especially interesting feature of this runniness is that it occurs in two distinctively different fashions. At all stages of manufacture, the dominant appearance is that of a bulk blob of material dribbling from the intended design line in a gravity-driven direction, which was downward during the firing. The second type of runniness, which occurred almost exclusively in all middle Rio Grande village pottery, but only after around 1600, serves as a useful clue to dating a vessel with this feature. The distinctive appearance of this second type of runniness is quite different from that of the bulk blobs, consisting of narrow, "watery" lines that boiled out of the bulk material and likewise ran in a downward direction. In both types of runniness, the direction of the lines indicates the vessel's orientation during firing, which usually was upside down.

The melting of the lead oxide and its resolidification into a fused and lustrous state qualifies this material as a true glaze. Thus much of the decorated pottery from San Lazaro and many other villages of the region is called Rio Grande Glaze Ware.

Upon firing, the clay and tempering material used to construct the pottery at San Lazaro results in a finely grained texture that is often pink or red, sometimes uniformly tan, and usually with a grey core in the middle of the vessel's wall. The grains of temper are mostly light in color, although some are dark brown or almost black. Despite the usefulness of material analysis in the identification of the pueblo of origin, we will not discuss this feature in our descriptions.

Indeed, the emphasis of our text is to describe the styles of form and design of the San Lazaro pottery, with less regard for the technical matters that are required for a complete analysis.

Thus, for example, we do not identify the various materials used to cover the surface of the vessels. The colors and placement of this slip material, however, can be indicative of style preferences of individual potters or groups of potters, and also might vary with such things as availability of material or, perhaps, even the season of manufacture. Therefore, we often comment on the color placed on the inside of jar necks, which can be red or white, or the extent of slip coverage near the base of the vessel, neither of which may be easily discernable from the photographs, but both of which may eventually be found to have cultural significance.

The sequence of our discussion is:

1. BOWLS	2. JARS
Standard	Regular
Shouldered	Handled
Flat-bottomed	3. OTHER POTTERY

The designs on San Lazaro pottery are almost invariably geometric, so that the rare examples with human or animal figures are conspicuous. An especially common figure is the black-edged-red path line, which encircles the vessel except for a small characteristic break, from which may sprout so-called "key" figures or variants thereof.

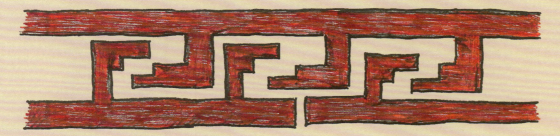

Figure 1   Path lines with attached key figures

Bowls

We commence with this form because bowls furnish the principal basis for both dating the sequence of styles and for naming each of the types. The characteristic features of standard bowls are not much incurvature of the rim and the presence of designs on both interior and exterior surfaces

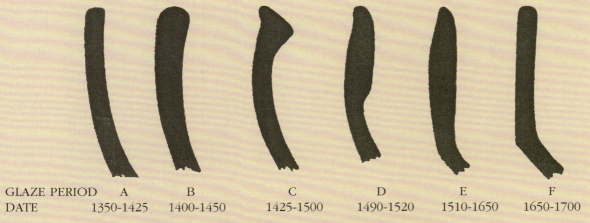

Figure 2   Rim forms on standard bowls

Figure 2 shows typical rim form cross sections for the six styles that are usually recognized. There is surprisingly minor variability at San Lazaro; most examples match one or another of the forms with little uncertainty.

In contrast, figure 3 illustrates cross sections of rims on typical shouldered bowls, most of which are likely to have been made during Glaze Periods D and early E at San Lazaro.

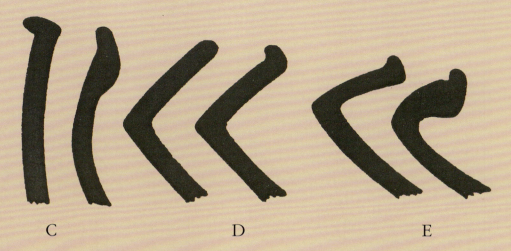

Figure 3   *Rim forms on shouldered bowls from San Lazaro*

Shouldered bowls with no decoration on the interior surfaces belong to this class of bowl. For each glaze period, different names relate to variations in form and/or design styles.

Standard Bowls

Some of the types of names for each of the glaze periods are the following:

Period A. Numerous type names including, for example, Cienegilla Glaze-on-yellow.
Period B. Several type names, including Largo Polychrome and Largo Glaze-on-yellow.
Period C. The most common name is Espinosa Polychrome.
Period D. The most common name is San Lazaro Polychrome, named for the village that is the subject of this book.
Period E. The commonly accepted name is Puaray Polychrome.
Period F. This type is usually called Kotyiti Polychrome.

In our discussions, we seldom use the type name, which is sometimes controversial, but instead simply refer to the glaze period letter.

There is an interesting but unresolved anomaly regarding the standard bowls from San Lazaro. Numerous standard-bowl fragments are scattered all over the surface and within the buildings, from which restoration or partial reconstruction cannot be accomplished with confidence. Among these fragments, most samples available have a remarkably high number of fragments from Glaze Period A—as many as from either Period C or Period D. Few bowls from period A can be reconstructed with confidence.

Furthermore, despite the occurrence of a significant number of bowl fragments that are typical of Glaze Period B, only one restorable bowl from that period has been discovered. For Glaze Period C, numerous fragments have been found, as many as from Period A. However, the only two restorable bowls from Glaze Period C are from very late in that period. Indeed, both of them are at the transitional boundary between Periods C and D, and would justifiably be included in either category. The following discussions refer to both the whole and restored examples illustrated in the photos.

Glaze Period A (ca.1350-1425)

A single small bowl, perhaps of Cieneguilla Glaze-on-yellow, the only available restorable example, is number 78 in the collection.

Bowl 78

Glaze Period B (ca.1400-1450)

The single example, a typical and handsome standard bowl, is number 25. An interesting feature of this bowl, the presence of a large red circular area at the exterior base, makes the type name, Largo Polychrome, seem appropriate (see plate 75, page 122).

Bowl 25

Glaze Periods C and D Transitional (ca.1500)

The two standard bowls from this transitional period differ significantly from each other. Number 29 is well made, but has no red in the designs. The entire surface, inside and outside, is covered with a thin, white slip. Both the interior and exterior designs consist of hooked figures on diagonal lines. The numerous diagonal dashes on the interior rim are unusual.

Bowl 29

The outstanding feature of number 22 is the pair of hands outlined with a poor quality of glaze that has altered to dusty, light grey. These figures are filled in with red slip, as is the interior path line from which they sprout. Figures that have been identified as birds emerge from the exterior path line. The overall appearance of rough surface finish, sloppy design lines, and distorted form are surprisingly at odds with the unusual nature of the interior figures that suggest a ceremonial significance deserving of careful execution.

Bowl 22

Glaze Period D (ca.1490-1520)

Most restorable standard bowls from San Lazaro are from Glaze Period D. Also illustrated are several examples that are not restorable, but are included because of one or another outstanding feature.

Bowl number 103, an example that is not confidently restorable, is decorated with a human face from which sprout arms that end in key figures with a possible interpretation of fingers, even in the absence of a face. Like bowl number 22, this bowl has a surprisingly sloppy design execution with a glaze material that has altered to a dusty grey color. The same face with hands also appears on small handled jar number 185 (see plate 175, page 247).

Bowl 103

A similar figure without a face also can be seen on bowl number 16. Designs on the interior of this bowl are quite faint.

Bowl 16

FRANCIS HARLOW AND DWIGHT LANMON

The design on bowl number 17 is positively identifiable as representing hands, much like those within bowl number 22. Again, the interior designs are rather faint. An unusual feature on the interior of the rim are the isolated, triangular figures with F-shaped extensions.

Bowl 17

Bowl number 104 is a reassembled vessel lacking restoration to fill in the holes. Both the isolated dashes on the exterior and the red-filled arcs in the interior are characteristic of pottery designs during Glaze Period D. Bowls 27 and 70 also are typical for the middle of Glaze Period D.

Bowl 27

Bowl 70

Bowl 104

Bowl number 97 is unusual, with an exterior appearance suggesting a relationship to Glaze Period D jar number 2 (see page 309). The interior surface is bisected into two fields of design, one with a cream slip and the other with a thin, much-eroded red slip. Numerous "X" figures in thin glaze decorate the red-slipped half of the interior even on the interior rim. The geometric designs on the cream-slipped half appear to be constructed of key figures and an occasional "X."

Bowl 97

The next three bowls, numbers 57, 36 and 37, have in common a straight or dogleg band across the interior as well as a different color for the exterior underbody from that of the exterior design area. The wide interior band has red slip and glaze designs in it. The exterior designs are also closely related, with fringed hooks either floating freely or else attached to a black-edged-red path line. The neat interior designs of number 36 also include stylized bird figures in the band below the unbroken path line.

Bowl 57

Bowl 36

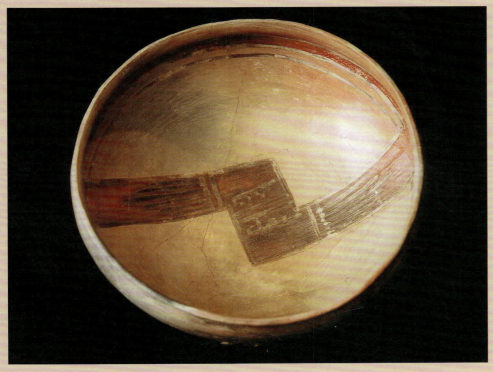

Bowl 37

Glaze Periods D and E Transitional (ca. 1520)

As the thickened part of the bowl rims got taller, Glaze Period D shifted seamlessly into Glaze Period E. Most of the following bowls that show the transition could be classed as either late D or early E.

Among the typical design styles that persist during this transition are the black-edged-red path lines that occur on the exterior of bowl number 66. The simple interior design on the bowl consists of black-edged-red arcs with red fillings attached directly to the red filling of the path line.

Bowl 66

Bowl number 26, however, demonstrates some innovations that characterize late Glaze Period D. On the exterior are found bird figures, with red filling attached directly to path line that has no break as it circles the pot.

Bowl 26

The rim on bowl number 56, which can be seen in cross section in the photograph, has a shape that is closer to Glaze Period D than to Glaze Period E.

Bowl 56

Bowl number 24 shows sloppiness in the application of the glaze material, especially in the interior designs. Large globs of glaze on the rim are also somewhat unusual.

Bowl 24

Beautiful bowl number 21 has an interior figure that does not have enough fingers to be a hand, so instead has been called a "capitan." The external design shows an unconventional adaptation of the black-edged-red path lines. On the exterior of this bowl is a reversal of the more unusual red slip lying below a cream slip in the design area. In this case, the design area has red slip and the area around the base is simply well-polished, clay and temper body material. The interior has a black-edged-red path line, with the unusual feature of a break without one of the end bars.

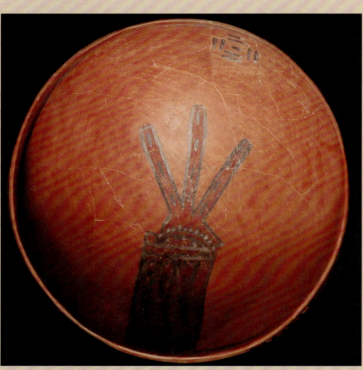

Bowl 21

Exterior of Bowl 21

There is some evidence that open-ended red areas are characteristic of pottery made at Santa Ana Pueblo from the late 1600s until about 1800.

Bowl number 38 also exhibits the absence of complete closure of black edging around red areas. On both sides of the bowl occurs a pattern with an open gap that appears to be intentional. The interior designs combine the features that also appear in Glaze Period D bowl numbers 97 and 37 (see pages 284 and 285).

Bowl 38

Bowl number 60 has an interior rim design like that on bowl 26 (see page 286). The exuberant exterior design may have Hopi Indian ancestry, perhaps because of migration of Hopis to a village south of Albuquerque called Pottery Mound, with the stylistic ideas later reaching San Lazaro. The thin, cream-colored exterior slip does not extend all the way to the base, a characteristic common to bowls of this age.

Bowl 60

Glaze Period E (ca.1520)

Two standard bowls have rim shapes that are characteristic of Period E.

Bowl A-2 clearly exhibits the change in design style that accompanies the transition from Period D to Period E. The common earlier use of exterior key figures has largely been replaced by more elaborate designs that often incorporate stylized bird figures such as those on this bowl. However, the black-edged-red path lines persist and continue until ca. 1700. On this bowl there are no breaks in any of the interior or exterior path lines

Bowl A-2

Inside of Bowl A-2

Remarkable bowl number 96 has thick red slip both inside and outside. While the exterior design style is nothing special, the interior of the bowl is decorated with a human figure with a kachina head carrying either a rattle or perhaps a bow with arrowheads that likely indicate the arrows that the figure intends to shoot. Unfortunately, the bowl is not sufficiently complete to show the entire form of the human figure.

Bowl 96

Glaze Periods E and F Transitional (ca.1650)

These four standard bowls, numbers 96, 23, 28 and 74, are more or less degenerate in design execution. Bowl number 23 is an exception insofar as interior decoration is concerned, having neat patterns in a well-controlled glaze. On parts of the exterior, the glaze has spread so badly that it has nearly obliterated the artist's intention, whereas other parts are quite neat. There is no red at all in the designs.

Bowl 23

Bowl number 28 also has a strong external flexure that is nearly a keel. The thick glaze edging of the simple designs shows some degree of uncontrolled spreading.

Bowl 28

Shouldered Bowls

These bowls are characterized by both the lack of interior designs and, with time, the progressively increasing incurvature of the rim. As indicated in figure 3, page 278, on shouldered bowls the external keel occurs well before it does on standard bowls.

Bowl number 74 is an example of the transition between Glaze Periods C and D. The only decoration consists of three "X" figures and a circumferential glaze line on the top of the rim.

Bowl 74

Bowl number 20, which seems slightly later than number 74, perhaps is a typical example from early Glaze Period D. Although it also bears "X" figures, they are part of a much more elaborate design band.

Bowl 20

Bowl number 75 has the typical form of Glaze Period D. There is a slight, but sharp keel in the external contours. The external white slip above the keel slopes down onto the underbody in a seemingly random fashion. While the generous application of glaze paint has resulted in considerable smearing of the design lines, the decorative intent of the artist remains clear.

Bowl 75

Typical for Glaze Period D, shouldered bowl number 72 has a distinct external keel. The glaze decorations on the exterior above the keel show better control of the material than on many of the other shouldered bowls.

Bowl 72

Shouldered bowl numbers 67, 68, and 106 are quite similar to each other. None has red slip on either the interior or the exterior surface, although on number 67 the external, cream-colored slip extends downward on the underbody about one-third of the way to the base. The glaze paint on number 106 is very thin and watery in spots so as to be almost invisible in the photograph. The watery material did not run in narrow streaks like those that appear of vessels made after ca.1600.

Bowl 67

Bowl 68

Bowl 106

Bowl number A-1 has a pinkish slip on the interior and an external glaze paint that was applied thickly to produce a noticeable texture and considerable smearing. This bowl is typical for Glaze Period D.

Bowl A-1

Bowl number 69 has a much greater slope of the area above the keel, which suggests a date in early Glaze Period E. While the designs are sloppy, the form is attractive.

Bowl 69

Bowl number 65 likewise has strong, in-sloping contours above the keel. The example is unusual for having a simple design in the interior, a cross that carries the only red coloring on the vessel. Again, early Glaze Period E seems like an appropriate assignment.

Bowl 65

The glaze decoration on the exterior of bowl number 30 does not clearly reveal the intent of the artist. Two small figures have been sculpted onto opposite sides of the bowl. One is a quadruped and, while the other was missing when the bowl was found, a nearby sculpted bird appeared to fit the rim scar in a way that suggests that it does, indeed, belong with this bowl (see plate 178, page 249).

Bowl 30

Bowl number 31 is elegant in its form and in the strong, red slip color on both the interior surface and the exterior underbody below the keel. There is evidence from the nature of the materials used to construct the bowl that it was made at some other pueblo and imported to San Lazaro. This example has by far the greatest flare near the lip of any of the shouldered bowls in the collection.

Bowl 31

Flat-Bottomed Bowls

There are two forms of flat-bottomed bowls—circular and rectangular. The two circular bowls are quite different from each other. Bowl number 71 is decorated with exuberance, both inside and outside, and the form is essentially cylindrical with a completely flat bottom and a flaring rim. The interior is slipped with a strong, red material, and the side walls are painted with two types of designs. One, probably representing birds, is solid pigment throughout. The other is a cross with bars on each arm.

On the flat interior bottom is one encircling band of glaze near the wall; the rest of that surface is unpainted. On top of the flared rim are numerous oblique dashes of glaze.

The outside of bowl number 71 has a thin wash of creamy slip on which are painted two black-edged-red path lines, neither of which has a break. Between them is a pattern of oblique zigzag lines with adjacent dots along some parts. This unusual bowl is handsome in its bold shape and distinctive decoration.

Bowl 71

In contrast, bowl number 77 is quite subdued in both its form and decoration. It suggests a relationship to the "soup-plate" bowl form made at many of the pueblos in the 1600s and early 1700s.

Bowl 77

Of the three rectangular bowls, two have stair steps sculpted on either two or four of the sides. On pueblo Indian pottery from many of the villages, this embellishment of form is believed to have sacred ceremonial significance.

Bowl number 99 was constructed and decorated with little care for precision in modeling or decorating. The exterior design contains "X" figures, but otherwise appears to have an essentially random layout of glaze lines (see plate 176, page 248).

Bowl 99

Bowl number 98 has an interesting relationship to bowl number 97 (see page 284) from Glaze Period D. Both have a bisection of slip into red and cream areas. Despite the crudeness of its glaze design, this bowl is quite handsome because of the dark intensity of its surface finish.

Bowl 98

Also see page 151

Bowl 98

Bowl 98

In contrast, bowl number 102 is plain in both sculpture and decoration. However, the "dragonfly" figure on the exterior is noteworthy.

Bowl 102

When found, the bowl contained corn and was stored in a large vessel under the floor of a room (see plate 79, page 126).

Bowl number 105, which is also quite plain, appears to have been constructed and decorated with indifference.

Bowl 105

Jars

Two very different kinds of jars are found at San Lazaro Pueblo. One of these, called a water jar or olla or *tinaja*, is typically 20 to 30 cm in height and rather elaborately decorated with glaze-paint designs usually containing red slip as filler. The other type of jar is small, usually around 10 cm tall, almost always with a pair of handles near the mouth, and decorated most often with simple, sloppy glaze figures that seldom incorporate red pigment. These small vessels have been called ceremonial, fertility or pollen jars, but we simply sort the two styles into regular jars and handled jars.

Because dating the glaze period for each jar is less direct than dating bowls, form and design style are employed for guidance with dating determined by similarities to bowls in decoration and to vessels from other sites in form.

Regular Jars—Early

During Glaze Periods A, B and C there is usually no flare at the rim; indeed, the neck is sometimes straight and vertical in profile. The interior of the neck is not slipped with red pigment, in contrast to the almost invariable use of red within the neck in Glaze Period D jars. The contour is rounded, rather than angular, at the position of maximum diameter, while the bottom framing line of the design layout usually lies above the point of greatest diameter. Generally, there is no red in the body designs, but this exclusion of red is not always confined to only the early glaze periods; it also is absent on jars of Glaze Period D and later.

The earliest of the restorable regular jars is number 32. Because on the bottom there is an unslipped area approximately 25 cm in diameter that is pinkish in color, the jar qualifies as a true polychrome. We are inclined to assign the vessel to Glaze Period B and to use the name Largo Polychrome.

Jar 32

Jar 48

Jar number 48 also has a pinkish area at the base approximately 30cm in diameter. The only qualitative difference from jar number 32 is the presence of a simple design on the neck. Again we use the name Largo Polychrome from Glaze Period B for this jar.

Jar 13

Jar number 13 is likely from Glaze Period C, for which the name Espinosa Polychrome is appropriate. Considerable stylistic evolution from jars 32 and 48 is particularly noticeable in the black-edged-red path line from which sprout oblique path line extensions terminating with key figures commonly used in Glaze Period D. Like the jars of Largo Polychrome, this example has no red slip within the neck, but in this case, the underbody is entirely red-slipped.

For jar number 35, the assignment to a glaze period is somewhat uncertain. Except for the noticeable outflare at the rim, we might have assigned the vessel to Glaze Period B or C, but the flare, with an almost beveled contour, is much more typical of Glaze Period D. Nevertheless, our current inclination is to include this jar in Glaze Period C, especially because of the lack of red in the neck, the rounded contours at maximum diameter, the placement of the lowest framing line above that position, and the sparseness of design on the body.

Rim Form

Jar 35

Jar number 3 appears to have been made at the transition from Glaze Period C to D. Only the absence of red slip within the unflared neck restrains us from suggesting a later time of manufacture.

Jar 3

Regular Jars—Glaze Period D

The overwhelming abundance of regular jars from Glaze Period D provides the opportunity to see the scope of form and decoration on these many fine examples of San Lazaro Polychrome. We have sorted and resorted these jars in a vain attempt to develop some systematic recognition of significant groupings of the variations that occur. We attributed significance to any of the variations, provided there was a consistent correlation with one or several other variants. However, the only correlation that seems to have significance is associated with the absence or presence of red in the mid-body designs. Often the absence of red seems to be associated with the more traditional design features for the type and can, we speculate, be associated with earlier dates of manufacture in Glaze Period D. Because the presence of red in the mid-body designs appears to be consistently associated with novel and experimental design elements, we speculate that it is associated with later dates of manufacture in Glaze Period D. These associations are not invariable, however, as the following descriptions show.

Regular Jars—Glaze Period D (with no red in mid-body designs)

Jar number 5 is a classic example of this type, with key figures sprouting from the path line at the shoulder. Jar numbers 5, 8, 10, 1, and 7 all have one or another form of diagonal pairs of figures that reflect each other, which suggests, because of their common occurrence in Glaze Period C pottery, that these vessels are early in Glaze Period D.

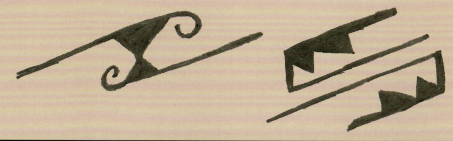

Jar 5

FRANCIS HARLOW AND DWIGHT LANMON

Jar 8

Jar 10

Jar 1

Jar 7

Jar numbers 33, 14, and 2 also have fragments of these reflective diagonals, but they are accompanied by a variety of other elements including fringes, zigzags and groups of multiple vertical lines.

Jar 33

Jar 14

Jar 2

Jar numbers 11, 42, and 44 have no black-edged-red path lines, except as parts of interlocking, but disconnected, figures on the neck.

Jar 11

Jar 42

Jar 44

Jar number 53 appears to have suffered considerable damage with both degeneration of glaze and an interior that looks burnt, like rough charcoal.

Jar 53

Jar numbers 12, 41, and 61 are unusual in having no black-edged-red key figures on the neck. Jar number 12 comes the closest to having these traditional figures, but here they have been modified from keys to birds.

Jar 12

Jar 41

Jar 61

Regular Jars—Glaze Period D (with red in mid-body designs)

Of this type two variations occur—those that have standard key figures and those that do not.

Jar numbers 4, 43, and 9 have more or less traditional key figures on their necks, but reflect novel experimentation in other ways, with fringed bow tie designs, zigzags with birds, bent parallel lines and exotic bird tails.

Jar 4

Jar 43

Jar 9

Jar numbers 39 and 6 have no black-edged-red key figures on their necks. Both do, however, have traditional black-edged-red path lines that persist on pueblo pottery until shortly after 1700, with occasional recurrences thereafter, for example, at Zia Pueblo. The glaze paint on both of these jars is more or less sloppy.

Jar 39

Jar 6

Regular Jars—Glaze Period E

The collection contains jars of both early Glaze Period E (up to and shortly after 1500) and late Glaze Period E (commencing ca.1600), with a major hiatus between them because the village was not occupied during that interval.

The early jars continue and extend the stylistic developments that occurred during Glaze Period D. Two of examples, numbers 49 and 51, even preserve a semblance of the older black-edged-red key figures on the neck. Distinctive features for early Glaze Period E are subtle and not necessarily completely consistent. Although the rim bevel is present on all four of our examples, more significant is the beginning of a new style of form and design layout as seen in figure 4 (see next page). While at this stage the new features are scarcely noticeable, a century later they become well established as, for example, on jar numbers 34 and 63 (see page 319). The essence of this style lies in the development of progressive isolation of the mid-body design band, which slides down to encompass the region of greatest diameter. Jar number 49 shows the early stages of this process especially well.

Rim forms

Jar 49

Jar 51

Figure 4

Glaze Periods D and E
1500-1600

Late Glaze Period E
1600-1650

Early Glaze Period F
1650-1675

Late Glaze Period F
1675-1700

Jar numbers 51 (see page 316) and 47 show that some potters still knew how to control the behavior of the glazing material. Both jars exhibit isolation of the mid-body design band from the neck decorations, although the mid-body design band on number 47 has not slipped down quite so far as it has on other examples.

The neck design and mid-body band are isolated from each other, with the latter lying close to the region of greatest diameter. This jar also shows another common feature for early Glaze Period E—the transition to sloppiness in design execution and use of much runnier glazing material.

Jar 47

Jar number 40 is different from the others in having a vertical bevel in the rim, no red in the designs or anywhere else on either the interior and exterior surfaces, and only a slight concavity in the vertical profile just below the lowest framing line (also see page 139).

Jar 40

Two examples from late Glaze Period E that show enormous changes from all the earlier jars in the collection are jar numbers 15 and 19, both of which were recovered in the historic part of the village and date after ca.1600. Neither has red in the designs, and both show the narrow fingers of a watery glaze fraction that is a strong indicator of manufacture during the 1600s. White slip extends from the rim down onto the underbody in a style that reverses the idea of a red slip extending part way down the underbody, as frequently occurs on jars from many other of the pueblos during the 1600s and persists until after 1900 at most of them. There is little resemblance to the jars of Glaze Period D, partly because of the passage of nearly a century and likely also because the new residents of San Lazaro included many whose ancestors came from other villages in the area.

Jar 15

Jar 19

Regular Jars—Glaze Period F

Two examples, numbers 34 and 63, represent the final stage of sculpture initiated by the Tewa Indians to the north in the late 1500s. The essential features of this form include a concave base (for both carrying on the head and for stability when set on a flat surface), slightly concave underbody slopes, a mid-body bulge that carries the principal band of decoration, a relatively tall neck, and a pronounced flare at the rim (especially on number 63). Significant glaze runniness, in both bulk and the thin, watery streaks of the 1600s, occurs both on these two jars and very commonly on Glaze F vessels from many other pueblos of the Rio Grande Glaze Ware area. The extension of white slip onto the underbody shows on both examples. Jar number 34 exhibits this extension as a white banding on the upper part of the underbody, a reverse-color mimic of the red banding seen at so many of the other pueblos.

Jar 34

Jar 63

Handled Jars

Relatively small handled jars have been found in several villages east of the Rio Grande and into the Galisteo Basin. Possibly each pueblo made its own in a style that was seen during visits between villages. Or possibly they were all made at one site and, being easy to carry, were exported as gifts or traded in exchange for other items of value. Most of the vessels are quite crudely constructed and decorated, and the use of red, either as a slip or as coloring within the designs, is rare.

Of the eighteen available examples, half have vertical handles and half have horizontal handles. The ones with vertical handles are numbers 175, 176, 179, 181, 183, 188, 189, 190, and 194. Those with horizontal handles are numbers 174, 177, 178, 182, 184, 185, 186, 191 and 193.

Jar 175

Jar 176

Jar 179

Jar 181

Jar 183

Jar 188

FRANCIS HARLOW AND DWIGHT LANMON

Jar 189

Jar 190

Jar 194

Jar 174

Jar 177

Jar 178

Jar 182

Jar 184

Jar 185
(see plate 175, page 247)

Jar 186

Jar 191

Jar 193

Noteworthy among these little jars with handles are numbers 185 and 186 because both have red in the designs. The most remarkable is number 185, which has on each side a human face from which emerge arms with key-figure terminations, likely representing hands. The overall appearance is much like that of bowl number 103 (see page 282), the only significant differences being the relative placement of the hands and the headdress or hair embellishments on number 185.

Jar number 186 appears to carry an overall red slip with a greater intensity of the color in the stair step figure. Also present on this little jar are two figures that may represent birds.

Jar 186

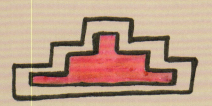

Other Pottery

These vessels of several kinds form a group of miscellaneous items that are not discussed in detail.

Vessel numbers 54, 100, and 101 are rough utility ware.

Vessel 54

Vessel 100

Vessel 101

Vessel numbers 50, 76, and 95 seem to have little relationship to any of the other pottery in the collection.

Vessel 50

Vessel 76

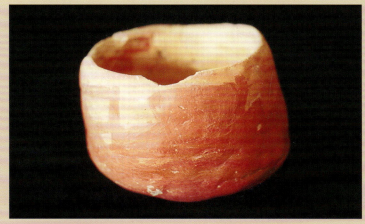
Vessel 95

Effigy figure vessel numbers 73 and 87 may be related to both the handled jars and shouldered bowl number 30 (see page 297).

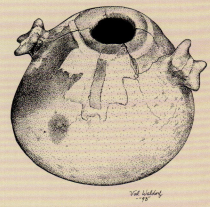
Vessel 87

Vessel 73

Imported from the Tewa Indians to the north, these two bowl fragments suggest commerce with tribes outside the immediate vicinity of San Lazaro. Bowl numbers 58 and 64 are late examples of Bandelier Black-on-grey, a type of pottery that is contemporaneous with Glaze Period D.

Bowl 58

Bowl 64

ACKNOWLEDGMENTS

I must thank many people for throwing their opinions and talents into this volume. It has been rewarding from the very onset of our excavations, as our thoughts and concepts began to develop and fall into place. Each artifact or strange new bit of information sent us into the research library and to experts in many fields. Every person we asked for information responded with more than we expected, or could use, in most cases. But most rewarding was the enthusiasm with which our friends and associates participated and wanted to be a part of our studies.

Several people should be singled out for their exemplary contributions: Charmay Allred, who can do anything, my daughter Kelly Sparks, who can, too, and Richard Blake, who is kind of the Godfather of this effort. Along with Lois Frank, these three took most of the photos you will see. Eric Blinman and Jan Orcutt, both superb professional archaeologists, helped us not only in the field, but also in the lab.

Those who helped us in the field are Nancy Bloch, Dee Breckhausen and his two sons, Mike and Zack, Dave Brewer, who also made some of the drawings for us, James Chatters, George Cox, who identified the plants, Susan and Perry Fishback, who don't take a backseat to anyone, George Frison, whose advice was always good, Mike Gramly, Elmer Guerri, Alan Hamel, Deborah Hofstedt and Little D, Mike Kammerer, Martha and Roland Mace, Stanley and Linda Marcus, Mika and Shiloh Old, Douglas Preston, Nancy Reynolds, William Shundt, Doug Schwartz, Suzanne Somers, William Turney, Jean Van Camp, John Ware, Jann Arrington Wolcott, George and Geri Zeimens, and all the kids from the Western Plains Historic Preservation Association, Inc, of course.

Experts in many different fields who helped us enormously include Gary Alkire, Keith Bakker, Kathleen Deagan, Jeffrey Dean, Emily Donald, Richard and Shirley Flint, Philip Fralick, Dody Fugate, Murray Gell-Mann, George Gummerman, Francis Harlow, Kathryn Jakes, Marcel Kornfeld, Stephen Kissin, Edmund Ladd, Charles Lang, Dwight Lanmon, Vicki Laszlo, Paul Logsdon, The Dog Lady, Tim Maxwell, Hope Merrin, Pamela McBride, Lori Pendleton, Donna Pierce, Thomas Polacca, Courtney Porreca, Stephen Post, Ann Ramenofsky, Barbara Riley, who helped us edit, Albert Schroeder, Franklin Shipla, Marion Schwartz, Joe Stewart, Kenneth Tankersley, David Hurst Thomas, Molly Toll, Rob Turner, Neil Weir, Laurie Webster, Kathy Whitaker, Tom Windes, and Barton Wright.

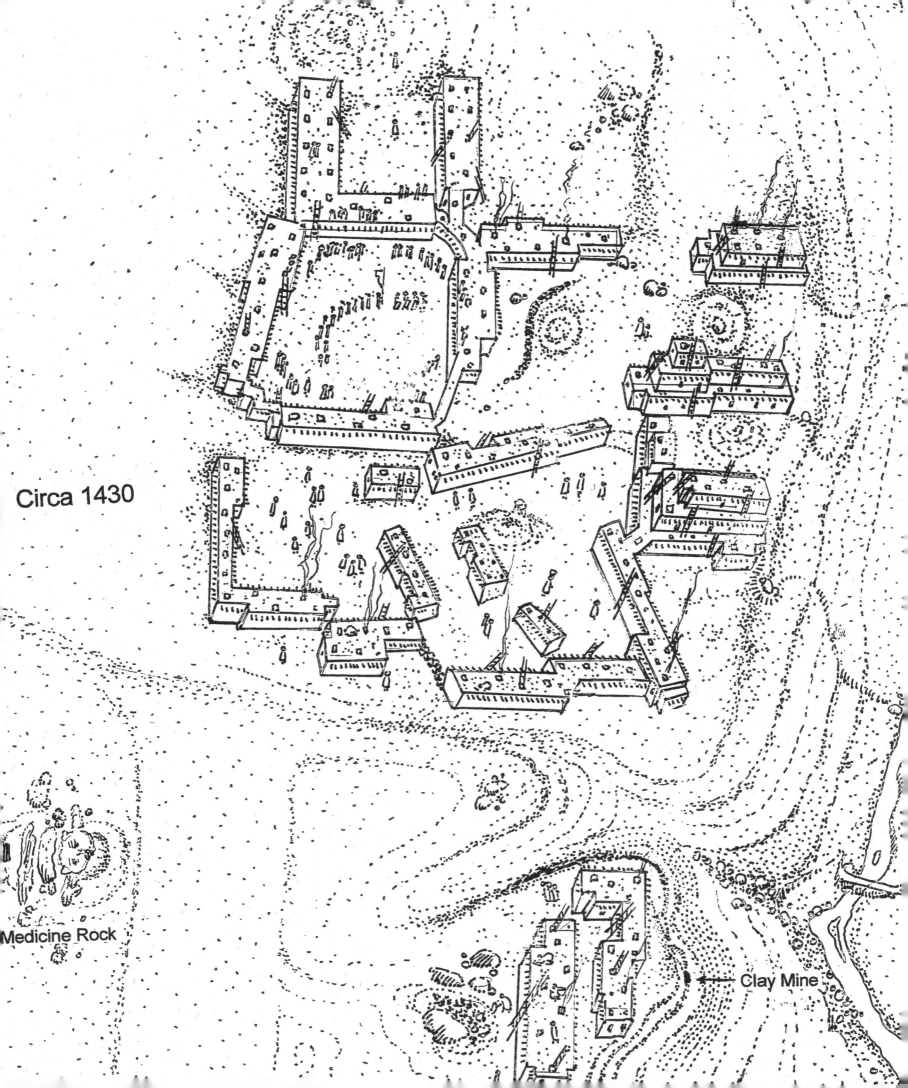